"Two pastoral counselors present a model of adult spiritual growth. They survey ancient and contemporary images of maturity, consider Christian virtue . . . and explore the relationship between power and intimacy in mature development. . . . The authors are especially perceptive about the roles of imagination and of absence in mature spirituality. The book is well-grounded in tradition, but thoroughly contemporary and original in its conclusions. Highly recommended."

Library Journal

"Throughout, [the book] never loses a sense of continued discovery in the Christian pilgrimage."

Bookstore Journal

"The authors explore issues of special significance today. . . . Particularly brilliant is 'Generous Absence,' the last chapter of the book."

Publishers Weekly

"The Whiteheads of South Bend have formed a partnership in many more ways than one. . . . This time the subject is maturing. They collate what is coming to be known about the subject and then present their own helpful angles. Part Two is particularly probing. . . . This realistic book imparts a sense of hope to motivate attention to 'strengthening,' in season and out of season."

The Christian Century

"The book is eminently readable and is especially helpful for those studying for the diaconate in the Roman Catholic Church. The book faces but avoids simplistic solutions to the often painful and angry struggle of the American Catholic Church. . . . The book is especially recommended for courses dealing with adult religious education, the Rite of Christian Initiation, the development of religious identity, and again, most especially diaconal preparation programs."

Sisters Today

SEASONS OF STRENGTH

SEASONS OF STRENGTH

New Visions of Adult Christian Maturing

Evelyn Eaton Whitehead
and James D. Whitehead

Saint Mary's Press
Christian Brothers Publications
Winona, Minnesota

The publishing team for this book included Carl Koch, FSC, development editor; Alan S. Hanson, production editor and typesetter; Stephan Nagel, art director; cover photo by Jack Hoehn, ProFiles West; pre-press, printing, and binding by the graphics division of Saint Mary's Press.

Chapter Ten, "Passages in Homosexual Holiness," originally appeared in *A Challenge to Love: Gay and Lesbian Catholics in the Church,* edited by Robert Nugent (Crossroad, 1983), copyright © 1983 by Evelyn Eaton Whitehead and James D. Whitehead.

Printed in the United States of America

Printing: 9 8 7 6 5 4 3 2 1

Year: 2003 02 01 00 1999 98 97 96 95

Library of Congress Catalog Card Number 84-4199

ISBN 0-88489-357-X

For
Jackie Trehearne,
mulier fortis,
sister and good friend

Contents

⋘ Preface ⋙

When *Seasons of Strength* first appeared almost a decade ago our intention was two-fold. Theologically, we hoped to continue the dialog between the rich tradition of Christian images of the spiritual life and contemporary models of human maturity, a dialog begun in our earlier work *Christian Life Patterns*. Pastorally, we were eager to explore themes that touched the real lives of real people: self-acceptance, anger, power, intimacy, authority, and sense of personal call.

The response to *Seasons of Strength* has been consoling, as comments from readers and reviewers have confirmed our own hopes for how the book could be helpful. In particular, we have been delighted to learn of the wide use this book has found in adult education settings and programs of adult formation in faith. Some examples:

• Participants in faith-sharing groups have used the reflective exercises at the end of each chapter to prompt discussion of how faith influences their family and work.

• Diocesan-based programs of lay ministry training have adopted *Seasons of Strength* as the initial text for incoming participants, drawing especially on the early chapters' developmental discussion of vocation.

• In religious congregations, vocation directors are recommending the book to persons considering religious life; formation directors use the book in joint-novitiate programs of preparation for religious vows.

• College teachers have found the book a useful text for introducing themes of Christian spirituality across the range of age and experience and religious sensitivity that characterizes undergraduate students.

• In masters' programs in university and seminary settings, faculty members use *Seasons of Strength* as a common resource to facilitate discussion in ministry reflection groups.

• Staff members of sabbatical programs serving returning missionaries and others experienced in culturally diverse pastoral settings have appreciated the cross-cultural relevance of the book's metaphors and images.

• In spiritual direction and retreat ministry, the book's discussion of the religious journey of homosexual Christians has been found particularly helpful.

We are grateful to Brother Carl Koch and his colleagues at Saint Mary's Press for their interest in returning *Seasons of Strength* to print. This edition retains the full text of each chapter, along with its reflective exercises. We have included a new annotated bibliography to bring the listing of additional resource materials up to date. We join with Saint Mary's Press in salute of those creative pastoral ministers whose work continues to build up the Body of Christ in these critical seasons of its strength.

EEW and JDW
July 1, 1994

Introduction

Vocation and Virtue

Christian adulthood is the focus of this book. In it we attempt to re-envision, to see anew, the patterns of power, confidence, and loss that shape maturity. This effort is guided by two ideas or, better, images that have long been central in Christian spirituality: vocation and virtue. Our goal is to befriend these images, to rescue them from narrow interpretations that have weakened each, to recover their power to illumine our adult journey with God.

A vocation refers, first and finally, to a sense that our lives are more than accidental, that we are "for something." Whether this intimation of purpose is murky or urgently clear, we find ourselves with an ambition to do something with our lives, to be somebody. In developmental psychology this sense of direction is being explored under various titles: a life project, a life theme, or the emerging personal "dream."

The Christian tradition adds to this psychological awareness the conviction that we are called. A human life does not happen randomly, nor does it proceed mechanistically with the genetic code as its only guide. Our lives unfold, as we sense ourselves being led, coaxed, invited into certain paths. Today this "call," the vocation by which we experience God's ambitious presence in our own lives, is being reimagined. The invitation to do something special with my life does not descend upon me from external authorities, appearing predominantly as a "should" or duty. It is inscribed within me, in my fragile gifts and my best insights. And it is more than my own invention. It has taken root through the influence of loved ones, the witness of communities, the force of cherished ideals.

14

This vision of a vocation suggests that it is not an elitist calling. Each of us is shaped by a confluence of our gifts and wounds and hopes—which, together, focus our lives along certain paths. Such a vision challenges that misinterpretation of the scriptural phrase "Many are called but few are chosen," which understands vocation narrowly, as limited to only a few in the community of faith. The deep passivity engendered by this restrictive view of a Christian vocation left most laypersons both uncalled and unchosen, with no special religious purpose in life.

There is another exciting change in the Christian image of vocation. We sense today that we are called not to a static "state" in life but to a journey. In my vocation I am invited in a certain direction, coaxed along a particular route or career (the word *career* itself means "path," or "trajectory of travel"). Christian vocation, rooted in our best and deepest hopes for our lives, leads us along certain careers, supported by particular lifestyles, focused on the promise of the Kingdom of God.

It is this vision of vocation that we explore in Part One of this book. Chapter One offers a new image for Christian maturity, suggesting that a vocation is to be "played" rather than worked. In Chapter Two vocation is discussed as the personal "dream" that can be fostered or frustrated by other ambitions active in the community. Chapter Three and Chapter Four trace the journey of a maturing Christian from child of God through the discipleship of young adulthood and into the stewardship of mature middle years. Part One concludes with a reflection on an implication of this journey. Maturing takes time: many seasons are required for that seasoning of instincts which marks us as Christian adults. We explore this process of seasoning in Chapter Five.

Part Two takes up our second theme, as we seek to recover the relevance of virtue today. For centuries of Christian understanding, virtues have been seen as strengths belonging to the "rational animal." This common image of the human person—reason managing our passions and animal desires—provided the boundaries for our understanding of virtue. Over the past generation this cultural vision has become less and less persuasive. Reason appears less regal than we had imagined; our passions seem more human than we had supposed. As this earlier model of the human person is set aside, its teachings about virtue have likewise been abandoned. We await a new vision, in the meantime unsure of the role of virtue in Christian life.

Our communal uneasiness with the topic of virtue has other sources as well. Since Freud we have become painfully aware of the many layers of motivation that influence human action. A desire for selfless service and an obsession with personal achievement can be bound together in our best efforts. Caring for an aging parent may be an exercise of filial devotion; it may offer, as well, a place to hide from the challenges of social interaction. Chastened by this insight into the ambiguity at the heart of our best actions, we have fallen silent about virtue.

A third factor contributes to the silence. In the midst of extraordinary cultural and religious change, we find that many of our learned habits no longer avail. Women and men are setting aside old courtesies and searching for new, more graceful ways of relating to one another. After Vietnam we are struggling for more mature modes of patriotism. In our churches, the shape of our devotional life changes as we explore new ways to worship together. In such flux, inherited habits do not always serve. Ancient patterns of interaction, once graceful, have grown rigid. Conventional behaviors often seem to obstruct rather than to assist growth. But there is enormous advantage to us, as individuals and as a people, in being able to rely on accepted patterns. When we set these aside, we flounder. We stumble as we search for new patterns that will serve the maturing of ourselves and our communities. Embarrassed by our awkwardness, we may well turn away from the very notion of virtue, judging it carries too much of the visage of the past to be of assistance to us as we face the future.

The attempt to recover Christian virtue begins in a new model of the person as the agent of virtue. Our image of the person is not as a "rational animal" but as a constellation of powers. Pictured not as a hierarchy, with one power (reason) guiding all the others (the passions), this grouping of powers functions more in partnership.

Sometimes in collaboration, sometimes competing, these powers are the energies that fuel the movement of maturing. It is this energy we examine in Part Two.

In Chapter Six we seek to recover virtue's original religious meaning as human strength experienced as gift. We then discuss several of the new faces of Christian virtue in contemporary life: the imagination itself as a potent resource on the journey (Chapter Seven); the virtue of self-intimacy as the growing ability to accept and to love the person I am being called to be (Chapter Eight). Anger has often been seen as an unwelcome intruder in Christian life; in Chapter Nine we investigate ways in which this volatile energy becomes a resource rather than a liability. Finally, in Chapter Ten we explore the virtues that are companions to a most disguised journey in Christian life: the maturing of gay and lesbian Christians.

In Part Three we confront issues of special significance for Christian maturity today. The first of these is power. To mature is to become more powerful; it is also to become more tolerant of our own enduring and even startling weaknesses. Maturity thus demands an increasing familiarity with personal power—its shape, its source, its goal. We consider these questions of personal power in Chapter Eleven. In Chapter Twelve we examine power in its social face, exploring the changing dynamics of authority and obedience in Christian life.

The final two chapters confront another central theme: intimacy. We examine the volatile interaction of women and men in the church today as a test of intimacy. And we conclude the book with a look at an unsuspected feature of adult intimacy, the experience of absence.

If the focus of this book is adult maturing, its central dynamic is the imagination. To change is to reimagine. Vocations fail when we cannot imagine that our lives have any special purpose or worth. Growth happens as we are able to foresee the next stage of the journey. Healing has a chance only if we can picture the possibility of forgiveness. The renaissance in Christian life today springs from the imagination: laypersons recognizing, with surprise, their own religious callings; women imagining a new potency; church leaders picturing a more mutual way of ministering in a community. We hold back a formal discussion of the imagination until Chapter Seven, but the influence of imagination is evident throughout.

Adult maturing and the imagination enjoy a special intimacy: it is in our images that we harbor our hopes and expectations about life. Some of these images are holy and invite us to growth; others are the twisted and compulsive demands that frustrate our development. But all live in the imagination. From this volcanic storehouse arise our terrifying nightmares, our inspired visions, our fantasies of failure and death. The imagination seems at once ally and enemy. It encourages our best efforts while, simultaneously, it casts shadows that remind us of frightening possibilities that may await. In our maturing we are invited to approach this ambiguous power within. In this book we explore this "approach" in the metaphors of taming, befriending, seasoning.

Central among the images of this volume are the play of a vocation and the seasoning of senses. Mature play includes an ability to "test the leeway" (Erik Erikson). This is a goal and promise of Christian adulthood: the mature strength to "test the leeway" in the traditional roles of Christian life so that we might hand these on, fresh and faithful, to the future. And the process by which such maturity is attained is the seasoning of senses, the gradual transformation of our instincts—of power and sexuality and justice—by the life and witness of Jesus Christ.

Finally, a word on how we hope this book will be used. We bring together here the social sciences and Christian theology in a dialog on themes of adult maturing. To these two conversation partners we invite a third—the reader. This volume is meant as a *practical* reflection on the maturing of the adult Christian. The life experience of the reader makes a critical contribution. We invite readers to confirm and to challenge the discussions here in the light of their adult journey. To help this process we have added reflective exercises at the conclusion of each chapter. Readers of our earlier books repeatedly tell us how useful they find these reflective opportunities. We hope that you will as well.

PART ONE

Images of Maturing: Ancient and New

Christians are exceedingly strange. Amid the random and conflicting events of our individual and shared lives, we detect pattern and purpose. We have this sense that we are called. Hard put to "prove" or even clarify this call, we nonetheless sense the invitation as we are lured to follow certain paths.

The Christian instinct about vocation leads us to imagine God's presence in everyday life, drawing us toward certain life choices. We are led toward specific commitments of love and work. We sometimes find our vocations confirmed in the strangest ways: in the detours of a career, in the fruitfulness of celibacy, in the gift of a retarded child.

The ancient conviction that God is about something special in our life is finding new and exciting expression today. In Part One we revisit ancient and contemporary images of the maturing of a Christian life. The goal is to reimagine the movement of God in our life as we explore a contemporary theology of Christian vocation.

1

The Leap of a Vocation

A quiet revolution is occurring in the land. Ancient distinctions between clergy and laity are giving way. A time-honored separation between Christians who have vocations and those who do not is being bridged. This is a revolution of the imagination: new visions of Christian life—of adult faith, of ministry, of community—are being born. At the core of this profound change is a reimagining of Christian vocation.

Every Christian is called. And we are called over a lifetime. The first conviction entails a nonelitist vision of a vocation. A Christian vocation is not a "specialty"; it refers not only to the priesthood or vowed religious life but to the particular direction and purpose that every maturing believer is expected to find and to follow. On "Vocation Sunday," then, we pray for all of us. It is when the sacrament of baptism takes root that a vocation is begun, as the believer embarks on a life journey toward and with God. This nonelitist vision of Christian vocations arises from a more vigorous sense of adult faith, and it will, in time, give new shape to the structures of Christian ministry.

If we are each called in different and particular ways, we are also called again and again. A vocation takes a lifetime. This insight gives vocation a more developmental sense. Our vocation grows and changes as we come into a fuller realization of our adult journey of faith.

A vocation is not a once-and-for-all call in young adulthood (to follow *this* career or enter *this* religious congregation). It is a lifelong conversation with God. Like any rich conversation, it is patterned by

21

periods of spirited exchange, times of strain and argument, and intervals of silence. In such a developmental vision of a vocation, fidelity is more than memory. Faithfulness entails more than recalling an early invitation; it requires that we remain in the conversation. Our fidelity must be mobile because the conversation continues.

A Christian vocation is a gradual revelation—of me to myself by God. Over a lifetime I gradually learn the shape of my life—and it takes a lifetime. At twenty-one, few of us could bear to learn all the turns and detours of the upcoming journey. Thus God reveals us gradually to ourselves. In this vision, a vocation is not some external role visited upon us. It is our own religious identity; it is *who we are,* trying to happen.

If a vocation is a lifelong invitation, we can see that it is an extraordinary exercise of the imagination. First, I *envision* my life moving in a particular direction. From scattered hints and uncertain inclinations, I begin to envision the shape of my life. I am, most often, brought to see this direction; this vision comes as a gift and sometimes as a command.

I not only envision the purpose of my life, but I must also *create* it. This is the second stroke in imagining a vocation. My life unfolds, demanding choices of love and work. It is in the face of these choices that I both receive my vocation and invent it. A vocation is not only vision; it includes my decision to live out this vision in the choices that give my life its actual shape.

An adult identity, like a Christian vocation, is an imaginative creation. I come to see—if I am fortunate—that the details of my life are more than haphazard or random. I may catch a glimpse of a design in the very particularity of my life—*these* parents, *these* abilities, in *this* place, at *this* time. There is a plot here! This recognition of a plot—a sequence in my life, a connection between my past and my future—becomes the core of an adult identity. *This* is who I am and what I am for. To come to this conviction is an exercise of the imagination. It is also the beginning of a vocation.

At the outset of adult life, the challenge—both psychologically and religiously—is to imagine what my life is to be about. In our senior years we are invited to affirm in retrospect the shape and goodness of this most peculiar plot. And during our middle years we can be required—by experiences of profound change or loss or stagnation—to reimagine the pattern and purpose of life. Sometimes reversals or disappointments tempt us to despair; there is no sense to it all. Hope eludes us, leaving us mired in this experience of "nonsense." Unable to picture a plot or purpose here, we may lose our way—both identity and vocation seem gone. It is imagination with its new visions of hope that can rescue us from this impasse. Thus we can come to see that vocations fail not when earlier visions undergo change but when we can no longer imagine that God is about something in our life.

The Creation of a Vocation

In the church today, we are involved in reunderstanding many of the images in which our faith has been expressed. The central image of creation is itself under review, as we recognize the many ways in which Christians have attempted to acknowledge our radical dependence before God. There are intriguing connections between images of creation and vocation. We will consider three images of creation here to see what they say to us about the reality of Christian vocation.

One way in which Christians have understood creation is as something that we *inhabit*. Here we imagine creation as God's production, but a production now fully accomplished. Ours is a world fully formed, fully imagined by God. In such a stable environment we see our lives guided by "natural laws," rules built in at the beginning. In such a vision, a vocation is likely to be seen as a clear role, stable and unchanging. As adults, we each inhabit a proper "state" in life, whether clergy or lay, married or vowed religious. Each is called to enter one of these vocational states and live faithful to its rules and guidelines. The role of imagination in such a vision is likely to be restricted to recognizing the state in life to which we are called. There is little enthusiasm for inventing new roles or improvising on those already given. Such inventiveness on our part would seem to suggest that God had been somehow negligent or mistaken "in the beginning."

A second vision that influences our understanding of vocations sees creation as something that is *worked*. Whether finished or still in process, creation here is imagined in the industrial metaphor of work. God created the world in a six-day (work) week. After the Sabbath rest, the enterprise was turned over to us. We creatures take up this work of creation in the "sweat of our brow." The chief feature of this image is its seriousness. We may participate in God's creation, but we do so earnestly and soberly. Purpose is a central value in such a model, leaving little room for experimentation or delight.

A third way to imagine creation is as something that is being *played*. This image of creation, which emphasizes inventiveness and delight, is an ancient one. Plato turned to this metaphor in his description of human nature: "Humans . . . have been constructed as a plaything of god and this is, in fact, the finest thing about them" (*Laws* 7.803c). Shakespeare wrote that "all the world's a stage" on which humans play out life. Both Plato and Shakespeare understood the play of creation as our performance of roles already fully scripted by a divine author. Play is thus essentially imitative: we find our joy in replaying divinely cast roles already given.

Recently, theologians have been exploring another interpretation of play, one that may allow us to reimagine more vigorously both creation and vocation. John Dominic Crossan and others suggest that a Christian theology of creation take more notice of play in its most creative aspect. In play (and so, in the play of a vocation) we do not simply repeat an already scripted role, we invent and improvise. When we play we do not just imitate, we also create.

Applying the image of play to creation itself, we can imagine creation as open-ended and in that sense unfinished. It is a creation still being played. We are participants in this creation, both replaying the classic roles and scripting new scenes in this continuing story. Past chapters give Christians guidelines for a plot that bears repeating. But it is an unfinished drama that demands our creative participation not only in response but in initiative and choice as well.

The image of creation as play is attractive in its creativity and delight, but it carries with it several inherent prejudices. Western culture bears three crucial biases about play: play has often been seen as childish, frivolous, and unreal. Childhood is judged to be the proper domain of play. Lacking full rationality and responsibility, children can only play at life. Once matured, adults should set aside play in favor of the duties and demands of their lifework. Artists and, in our culture, athletes may continue their preoccupation with "child's play," but they serve the rest of us not as models but as refuges from the serious business of adult life.

A second bias against play is that it is frivolous; we depart from weighty, adult matters by "playing around." In the Book of Exodus there is a passage that uses play in this pejorative sense. Describing the idolatry and immorality of the people during Moses' absence, the account notes that "after sitting down to eat and drink, the people rose up to play" (Exodus 32:6). The suggestion here is that play is not just some harmless distraction but an excess that turns the people away from Yahweh. For serious Christians, too, play has often been interpreted pejoratively. It is always a trivial pursuit, sometimes even sinful.

In a third bias, play is understood not only as childish and frivolous but as unreal. The Latin word for play, *ludere,* survives in our own word *illusion.* To play is to pretend, to occupy a fictitious role. To play is to step out of reality, to impersonate and even deceive.

With these cultural biases alive among us, we may wonder if play can be rescued as an image of creation and vocation. To undertake such a reimagining of play we need authorization. Are there any hints in the Scriptures that may help us envision play in its more positive and creative meanings? A clue may be found in the Book of Proverbs. Here we encounter Wisdom, the feminine form of God, describing her role in creation:

> I was by his side, a master crafter, delighting him day by day, ever at play in his presence, at play everywhere in the world, delighting to be with the children of humanity (8:30–31).

Innumerable questions, linguistic and theological, surround this strikingly non-Israeli picture of creation. Who is Wisdom, this companion and player with the Creator? Hebrew texts differ, some translating the first description as "master crafter," some as "child." The choice of child settles a number of issues: the Creator's companion would be a playful child, not an adult partner who might be construed as a consort. But apart from the suggestion of a feminine partner in the process, this story suggests connections among creation, play, and delight. Creation here is neither the serious work of an industrious maker nor the solitary invention of a bachelor god. It is rather with companionship and delight that creation is played.

Vocation as a Leap

If we can imagine creation as still being played—with us as players and partners with God, with the final act not written—then we are better able to envision the play of a vocation. This reimagining will demand that we toughen and expand our notion of play, rescuing it from both pious sentiment and cultural bias. A useful guide here is psychologist Erik Erikson, in his book *Toys and Reasons.*

Erikson takes up Plato's suggestion that play originates in the random leaps of the child. He then points to three distinct elements of these gratuitous and energetic bounds. First, the child leaps out of delight. For no special purpose ("except," the harassed parent may counter, "to drive me crazy!") the child leaps and jumps repeatedly. Performed simply for the delight of it, the leap is for its own sake.

Second, such a leap is a move against gravity. The child, in Erikson's phrase, "tests the leeway," challenging the gravity and givenness of life. If play is part delight, it is also assertion and contest.

Third, to leap is to fall. To launch oneself upward is to undertake an effort that will inevitably bring one back to earth. Fallings and failings seem essential aspects of the leaping that is play. Delight, testing the limits, falling—these ingredients of human play are also elements of a maturing vocation.

A vocation is a leap: we often speak of such a significant life choice as a leap of faith; sometimes it can feel like a leap in the dark! In a moment of life commitment, I "go beyond" the information available and give myself to something that escapes my sure control. How can I be sure that I should marry this person or join this religious congregation or pursue this career? Committing ourselves in these ways, we are likely to sense the risk—even the foolhardiness—of such a venture. And yet we want to make the leap. As young adults, we sense that we need to leave the familiar confines of our families and our own adolescent selves and set out for parts unknown and untested. Idealism and romance help propel us into the commitments that mark our twenties. And, like the child, we need to leap—to risk—again and again if we are to keep our vocations lively. In a developmental understanding, we see a vocation not as a one-time leap that lands us safely in the middle of a stable vocational state, but as an ongoing exercise of commitment that requires agility and grace.

A Leap of Delight

We may imagine a vocation as a leap, but how is it a leap of delight? One's vocation is a path to be followed in pursuit of the Lord. Most of us might agree that a vocation lived faithfully should be satisfying, but "delight" still feels foreign. This aspect of play seems difficult to incorporate into an image of a Christian calling. If we have grown up in the belief that holiness comes in sober obedience to the "shoulds" and "oughts" in life, there may be little room to see our vocations as delightful. The delight of a vocation is rooted in a sense of its goodness and "fit." I delight in the shape that my own life takes as I experience the way it fits my own particular gifts and limits. It is not just the *right* thing for me to do with my life, it is *good* for me as well.

How is a Christian vocation "for its own sake"? This element of play is not easily celebrated in a religious tradition steeped in a profound purposefulness. In marriage we make love in order to have children; our religious and priests live celibately so that they can serve better; we strive to live virtuous lives in order to merit heaven. With these good purposes so much a part of our sense of adult commitment, how can we experience our vocations "for their own sakes"? It may help here to recall the experience of liturgy, so central in Christian communal life. Liturgy, as our celebration of the Lord's enlivening and healing presence, is for its own sake. Romano Guardino has observed that liturgy is "pointless, but full of significance." Celebration arises among us in counterbalance to work and achievement. It is not, finally, *for* something else; it is for its own sake. But if our religious awareness of creation is couched exclusively in images of work and achievement, it will be difficult to envision the ongoing creation of our own lives as entailing celebration or delight.

Finally, the awareness of a vocation as a leap of delight must be more than theoretical. I must be able to savor my own vocation, to delight in the design that emerges as my life moves with God. In each vocation, whatever its shape, there is challenge and pain and stress. But a vocation holds more than this; we know the reward of accomplishment, the joy of presence, the comfort of peace as well. My appreciation of my own vocation deepens as I am able to name its delights for me. It is here that I celebrate "for its own sake" the shape that my life has taken.

Testing the Leeway

If a Christian vocation begins in a leap of faith and matures through a series of graceful bounds, it also "tests the leeway." This aspect of play reminds us of the limited mobility of our lives. The child's leap is purposeless, but it does have an inner economy: to see how high she can go. Gravity restricts how far she can jump, but it doesn't keep her from leaping. Erikson finds in this aspect of play a model of human maturity. We always find ourselves in a context of limited mobility. The limits of our own abilities, the constraints of the environment and the historical setting—these restrict us. It is within, sometimes even against, the boundaries of these givens that we leap. It is in the interplay of possibility and limit that our vocations take shape. With no sense of limit, our lives lack definition and responsibility; with no feel of mobility, they grow stagnant and unplayful.

That a Christian vocation is an arena for such maturing interplay seems especially clear. The lifestyle I choose—married person, single adult, vowed religious, priest—has been chosen many times before in Christian experiences. As I live out this role I experience both its limits and its flexibility. I am not a priest or a married person "in general"; I am *this* priest, *this* spouse, *this* particular adult—my own version of this traditional role. Our vocation matures in this testing of the limits as we experience the tension between the limits that define our chosen roles and the flexibility that our own gifts and insights bring to them.

The church today is alive with this testing of leeway in our vocations. As a people, we are exploring whether the role of community leader will flex enough to allow married people to serve in this way; gay and lesbian adults are pursuing lives that are both genuinely Christian and fully sexual; women are challenging the male limits of hierarchical leadership. If these are examples of serious struggle, they are also instances of creative play. In the assertive interplay of these encounters the church's vocation is itself being tested and matured. In our resolution of these contests we are writing the next chapter in the church's history; we are playing out an as yet unimagined future.

We are reminded here how robust play is. It is more than frivolity or mere diversion; its fruits are more than simple delight. A Christian vocation demands that we be energetic and assertive players, willing to contest, able to push against the limited mobility of our religious heritage. Without this interplay, without the jostling and contesting involved, the tradition will stagnate. In the interplay of our vocations we enliven both our own lives and the life of the church. We play out in our own lives the sacred story of Jacob wrestling with Yahweh, as together they grappled toward a new, more mature relationship.

Falling and Failure

The vigor of this contest brings us to the third aspect of play: falling. Here again we learn that play is not without its lessons; we are reminded that in leaping we must be prepared to fall. In the rough-and-tumble of play the child learns that to fall is neither disastrous nor disgraceful. In fact, it is an integral part of the leap. The challenge for both the child and the maturing adult is to allow room for the fall. How do we learn to fall gracefully in our vocations?

This question brings us to a theology of failure. As Christians, with our special sensitivity to "the Fall," we have been reluctant to imagine failure as having a place—perhaps even a necessary role—in the maturing of vocation. If creation is a "finished product," there is little room for mistakes. Failure is easily identified with infidelity, and falling with sin. In Christian spirituality the ideal of perfection has made its special contribution to the crippling of play. To play is to chance falling; if falling is always moral failing, there seems little justification for Christian play. And many Christians have come to such a sense in their vocations. Finding themselves in roles that are stable but inflexible, they are unable to play because there is no place to fall.

There are, however, some clues in our religious tradition concerning a theology of failure. In our Easter liturgy we recall the original fall as a *felix culpa,* a happy fault. How can a failure of such tragic proportion be construed as happy? Its happiness is, of course, that it brought Jesus Christ into our midst. Through the Fall, God has become tangible to us. Ironically the Fall itself has become graceful. Tragic though it was, the Fall was also profoundly fruitful. In retrospect it even appears integral to God's loving design.

We can come to sense the place of fall in the play of our own lives as well. As our vocations mature, we experience the fruitfulness of failings. Every adult life is generously scarred with failure. In our love, in our work, things have not gone as we had hoped. Sometimes we were at fault; sometimes others seem to have been to blame; sometimes it "just happened." Early on we tend to respond to such failure with anger, regret, shame. In midlife we may come to see these events in a new perspective. In the graceful light of retrospection, we realize that these happenings were not just hurtful. Our wounds have contributed in strange but tangible ways to the substance of our vocations. A failure at an aborted early career helped turn me to my present work. Or the loss of an important early love I see now as a necessary, if painful, part of my maturing in intimacy. Such midlife reconciliations invite us to embrace and welcome these falls as genuine parts of who we are. We are able to celebrate the shape of our vocations, knowing both the strangeness and the goodness of our lives with God.

A maturing vocation likely brings another experience of failure. This is what we might call a developmental "fall from innocence." The first leaps of a youthful vocation, energized by idealism and romantic vision, often include high expectations of a church without flaw and a religious tradition without ambiguity. As we mature in the church we may be felled by the failings and shortcomings—even the sinfulness—we find there. This disillusionment functions as a developmental parallel to the painful but necessary realization in adolescence that "my parents are not perfect." The illusions that were necessary and useful to our biological and ecclesial childhood must fail us if we are to mature. How else will we know to put them aside? When we can acknowledge the necessary failure of these illusions, without simply resorting to bitterness and blame, we gain a more mature tolerance for ambiguity and error. The ideological vigor of young adulthood is softened as we play through the failures that are part of a maturing vocation.

At this point we can begin to reimagine what it means to be a graceful player. Mature play does not include rising above all mistakes; it does entail learning to fall gracefully. The acrobat or the gymnast might serve as a model of one who has learned to fall well. When she comes down "wrong"—turning an ankle or landing on her head—the acrobat learns to bounce up with a flourish as though the fall were part of the act. And, in the larger sense of play, it is.

But every metaphor limps. Sometimes it is best *not* to leap up and go on as if nothing has happened; some falls demand immediate attention and take time to heal. These falls remind us of the importance of the environment to our vocational play. If we leap, we need a safe place to land.

A Place to Play

Our discussion so far may give the impression that Christians play their vocations privately or in solitude, but the maturing of a vocation is influenced by the places where we play. Community is the context of vocational play; it is the Christian community that is our privileged playground.

British psychiatrist D. W. Winnicott has studied the first environment of human play, the relationship of child and parent. It is in this earliest interplay that the child develops a sense of self distinct from the parent. The child learns here the earliest lessons of intimacy by playing before and against this nurturing person who is "other" but trustworthy. Such a parent allows the child to leap, giving boundaries and rules that can be tested, and supporting the child when she falls. One of Winnicott's special contributions to a theory of play is his observation of the connection between trust and concentration. Only in a trusting environment will the child be able to give full attention to play. Without this concentration the child is too distracted to play well. With it she learns "to be alone in the presence of another." This ability is the foundation both of the mature play of Christian prayer and of the lifelong interplay of friendship and marriage.

Winnicott's brief observations help us appreciate the role of a Christian community as a trusting and trustworthy environment. Such a community—whether parish or family or religious congregation—provides the place to play out a vocation. It encourages leaping; it gives boundaries, rules, resistance against which individuals can test their own life choices; it offers a place to land.

We speak more colloquially of needing "a place to crash." We mean somewhere to come down after our daily leaps, a place that provides solid footing or cushioning arms for our descent. An unsupportive community resists this. It interprets leaping as restlessness and instability. It sees testing the leeway as ingratitude or infidelity. It responds to our falls with embarrassment or blame. In this kind of community, our leaping comes to a halt, or we go next door to play. Such a community stagnates in seriousness and self-defense. On the other hand, the trusting community has managed to learn the meaning of play, probably by recognizing its own leaps and stumbles. A flexible and safe place to play, a community of this kind fulfills its function as a sacrament. It is a sign of the continuing play of God's creation, a witness that Wisdom continues to "play everywhere in the world, delighting to be with the children of humanity."

Finally, it is in a trusting community that we learn the profound connections among play and trust and intimacy. In *Adaptation to Life,* George Vaillant summarizes this interplay:

> It is hard to separate capacity to trust from capacity to play, for play is dangerous until we can trust both ourselves and our opponents to harness rage. In play, we must trust enough and love enough to risk losing without despair, to bear winning without guilt, and to laugh at error without mockery. (p. 309)

As we tame failing and falling, we become mature players in our vocations. Better able to risk and test and fall, we show the next generation of believers the style of Christian play. We witness that a vocation is a lively, fragile, flexible gift to be played with energy. And in the interplay we predict the shape of Christian community for the future.

Reflective Exercises

You are encouraged to take a few moments in a quiet place, away from distractions, to reflect on the special movements of your own life. After some moments of quieting yourself, let the following questions arise within you:

1. With what kind of leap did my own vocation, my own adult Christian life begin?
2. Where do I continue to delight in my life, as good for its own sake?
3. Where am I testing the leeway in my adulthood? How do I experience the tension between the "roles" in my life and my own unique way of living them out?
4. What "falls" have been an important part of my maturing? Are there failures or mistakes in my past that I can recognize, in retrospect, as "happy faults"?

2

Christian Maturing:
The Story of Three Dreams

A Christian vocation is not an elitist calling but an invitation to make something good and holy of our life. The path may lead me to marry or remain single; it may lead me into the business world or a service profession or the priesthood. Whether loudly or barely heard, it is always a call that draws us to use our abilities to follow Christ's witness of challenge and care for the world.

In this lifelong conversation with God, we continue to hear hints and rumors of who we might become or what we are to do. Only gradually, over many decades, do we come to glimpse what God imagines our life might become. Testing our insights and hopes against our abilities and environment, we very gradually come into our vocations. A vocation is thus not a mystical or abstract notion; it is the changing shape of our adult lives as Christians.

This maturing of our hopes and commitments expectably takes a lifetime. In our forties we learn things about our strengths and weaknesses that we could not have known in our twenties; in our seventies we are still being revealed to ourselves. It takes a lifetime for God to show us who we are. Fidelity to a vocation, as we noted in Chapter One, is not just an act of memory. It is the decision to remain in the conversation. Continuing to communicate with God, to listen for God's voice in the successes and failures, delights and disasters of an adult life, we are more surely revealed to ourselves.

Our vocations mature through the revelations and purifications of such a lifelong conversation.

This developmental vision of a Christian vocation brings it into dialog with Daniel Levinson's notion of the "dream." In *Seasons of a Man's Life*, Levinson explores adult growth as a development of a dream or life ambition. Here, a dream is not a nocturnal fantasy but a life project—an enduring and growing sense of what I am to do in life. This dream is what I most want to do with my life. Such a life ambition runs below every specific plan and job; it struggles to survive every change and detour in adult life.

A Vocation as a Dream

A dream, and a vocation, is what I want to do "when I grow up." The five-year-old who wants to be a truck driver or a nurse or an astronaut gives an early hint of the dream. In our late teens and early twenties the dream emerges, often with much vigor. Readying us to enter the adult world, our imagination fills with ambitious plans or tentative hopes. Levinson's research recalls a special feature of the early dream: its idealism. The young woman wants to become not simply a doctor but a pioneering neurosurgeon; the young man wants to become not merely a writer but an award-winning novelist. The devout young Christian's ambition may be not only to help others but to travel as a missionary to poverty-stricken peoples in far-off lands. Psychologically, we need the energy of such idealism to propel us into the complex and confusing world of adulthood. The coming decades will see a mellowing of this idealism as our dream comes to fit us better.

During our twenties the dream undergoes much testing and renegotiation. On the inside we ask, Am I up to such a vision? Do I have the stuff to live out this vocation? And on the outside we are testing: Will the world allow me to do this? Is there room in the church for such a dream? With enthusiasm or tentativeness we try out our dreams, test our vocations in the real world. Sometimes this testing demands that we clarify a dream that is powerful but vague. The young woman wants to serve others, to help humanity—but how? What specific path is this desire to follow? Another young person finds himself with a powerful and very clear dream: to be a teacher. But experience, in school and elsewhere, begins to indicate that the dream will not be realized in this specific form. He is challenged to reinterpret his dream. How can his goals find expression in another career? What ambition lies under this specific vision of service and care? For many young adults the decade of the twenties is spent testing out these early dreams.

But something else may happen during this critical time: the dream may be lost. My dream, my vocation, abides in my imagination. Without nurturance it can wither and disappear. Either from lack of support or because we ourselves cannot believe in them, our dreams may be set aside. Confused or frightened, I may abandon the dream. One way out, which makes my abandoning the dream easier, is to find someone else who seems to have a strong sense of purpose—a spouse or leader or religious congregation—and join my life to that person's or congregation's dream. Or I may settle for living out the dream that a parent or teacher has for me. It may be decades later that I come to realize what I have done. At this point I am invited to an important and probably painful reconciliation with my own lost dream.

Before examining these reconciliations of midlife, we will consider some connections between the psychological notion of a life's dream and Christian convictions concerning vocation. First, each is understood as an expression of my deepest and best hopes for my life. They also share a common habitat: the imagination. It is in images that we envision our dream and our vocation. Whether these are "just fantasies" or realizable hopes will take time to determine. But we have vocations and life dreams only if we are attentive to the imagination. For Christians, both dreams and vocations are vehicles of revelation. The Old Testament is filled with stories of dreams and visions in which our ancestors recognized God's will for them. In the visions and hopes that make up our vocations, we—like they—learn who we are to be; we are revealed to ourselves. Finally, a vocation differs from a dream in a special way: a vocation is a dream personalized. A dream is often explained in terms of factors of environment or heredity. As Christians we believe that a vocation involves more; it is God's dream for us. Rooted in more than chance or fate, our vocation is what God has in mind—or better, in imagination—for us. In my vocation I am being imagined by God; God's dream for my life comes gradually to light.

Reconciliations with the Dream

In our twenties we explore and test the dream, making the choices that launch it toward realization or decline. I choose a career; I marry this person; I enter religious life. These commitments set us in pursuit of certain life ambitions. Usually in our thirties we are preoccupied with the work that our dreams demand: raising children, working at our ministry, building up an adult sense of competence and stability. Over these first decades of adult experience, we are fully involved in making something of ourselves—we are living out the dream, following a vocation. We are accumulating the information and insight into ourselves that may eventually lead us to reassess our dream.

In midlife many of us find ourselves reexamining our dreams. A vocation, a dream, is an ongoing revelation; it is to be expected along the way that we feel the need to revisit and reevaluate the direction our lives are taking. This "return" of the dream, which demands special attention in midlife, is part of the maturing of a vocation. It plays an important role in what our colleague J. Gordon Myers calls "the purification of expectations."

This reconciliation with the dream in midlife can take different shapes. In a first pattern we may be invited to come to terms with the way our dream has gone. Here the challenge is one of fit: to appreciate the ways in which my earlier dream, idealistic and grand, has found its more realistic shape in my life. I have not become all I hoped for; I may not have achieved the extraordinary visions of youth. But I have become this particular, if peculiar, version of the dream. In a mood of mellowness I am invited to embrace *my* life and *this* vocation, rather than an earlier and perhaps more grandiose version. The invitation in this reconciliation is, in Levinson's terms, one of "de-illusionment." Not disillusionment, but de-illusionment: we are called to let go some of the necessary illusions of youth. By now these illusions—about my talent or resourcefulness or influence—should be less necessary. As I become more comfortable with the shape of my own life, I can let go of self-descriptions that are more ideal than real. More self-accepting, I can rejoice in who I am becoming, even while mourning parts of the dream that will not be realized. This reconciliation is one face of a midlife purification of expectations.

A second kind of reconciliation may be demanded as I recognize the tyranny of the dream in my life. In our twenties we may give ourselves to a life ambition—with a vengeance. We are ready to sacrifice everything else to reach our goal, whether it is success or fame or even holiness. And we may even achieve it. But by midlife a dream so compulsively pursued is likely to have become a tyranny. Under its sway we have sacrificed too much—friends, family, health, peace of mind. We pray now to be delivered from the curse of our success. Reconciliation with a dream demands rescue from its tyranny. I am invited to recover parts of my life that I have ignored or denied in the all-out pursuit of narrow goals. I am reminded that a dream is but part of me; when it becomes a tyrant, it destroys other aspects of my life. In this reexamination I am called to forgive myself. Self-blame and guilt may be strong as I realize what I have done to myself. Forgiveness is part of the reconciliation demanded now.

In a third reconciliation we may be called to recover a dream deferred. This challenge occurs when I recognize that I have lost an earlier dream. I may have set it aside as I took a temporary job to meet the financial needs of my family; twenty years later the temporary job continues. Or I may have been talked out of my dream by a parent or someone else who judged it to be foolish or impractical. Now at forty-five or fifty, I sense this forgotten dream arising anew, asking again to be heard. Here too forgiveness is central to the reconciliation. As the dream returns I am tempted to blame myself or, more likely, "those others" who kept me from my dream. To recover this lost dream I will need to forgive this part of my past. If I cannot forgive, much of the new energy of the returning dream will dissipate in anger or regret.

In midlife the lost dream returns to a life that is intricately connected with the lives of other people—family, colleagues, companions. No longer the unencumbered youth to whom the dream first announced itself, we are bound with the commitments of the past several decades. Is there room for a new dream in such a life? Do the responsibilities of my previous choices crowd out any possibility of new choices, new directions for my life? In this reconciliation I am asked to introduce the returning dream into the network of my existing commitments. In the vigorous dialog that is likely to ensue, I try to re-envision and revise my vocation.

Another kind of reconciliation, not reported in Levinson's research, is witnessed in Christian communities today. This is the end of one dream and the beginning of another. An earlier dream has been achieved; narrow or not, it has been lived out. Now in midlife, new ambitions, perhaps not even imaginable in an earlier church, are being born within me. New revelations are being heard; a new stage of the journey with God begins if I can let myself hear the new voice of God and, with fidelity, follow it. This more radical breaking in of a new dream reminds us of the importance of our social context. Dreams do not arise in isolation; Christians do not receive vocations in private. As the church and our communities change and mature, new dreams are set loose.

A Community's Dream

Personal vocations are imbedded in social contexts. Our dreams begin within our families. They are nurtured or frustrated in neighborhoods, parishes, and schools—those settings where we learn what to expect from life. These places are themselves more than just a collection of individual dreams. A social setting, especially a family or a parish, can have a dream of its own. A group's special purpose, its shared ambitions and goals, can be recognized as its corporate vocation.

The family is the original arena of our dreams. Parents are busy not only with the pursuit of their own life ambitions but with fostering their children's dreams. An inner discipline that as parents we must learn to practice is to distinguish our own hopes from the fragile, beginning dreams of our children. Parents come to know, sometimes slowly and painfully, the hard truth of Christian stewardship: in our children we are the nurturers of dreams, the guardians of vocations that we neither control nor fully understand.

But a family is more than a collection of individual vocations. A family gradually develops its own collective dream: this group of people, responding to the many invitations of God that have both brought them together and put them in tension with each other, slowly forges its own set of values and hopes. The lifestyle and decisions that give this family its uniqueness also define its dream of Christian life. Such a family dream is often fragile. The busyness of everyday life can distract us from one another; we often seem to lack the time to share our deepest hopes. And so our sense of common aspiration can be lost or at least rarely celebrated. Or a family dream can be warped, with the ambition or needs of one member serving as constraint on all the others. But a family in which a Christian dream is alive fulfills the rhetoric of our faith: the family becomes a "domestic church."

Just as a Christian family matures in the development of its dream, so too a Christian community grows as it becomes aware of its own vocation. A parish, for example, expectably builds a shared sense of Christian purpose. How does such a corporate vocation arise? In its public actions, a community hands on some version of the Christian dream, whether as an exciting hope or as a withered memory. In every liturgical celebration and educational effort, a faith community announces its dream.

The religious development of the members of the community depends on this shared dream. Until recently, "religious formation" has usually referred to the initial training of vowed religious or priests. Yet formation of its members in faith is what any faith community must be about. And the vitality of the community's dream is crucial in this religious formation of all its members.

In religious formation, a faith community invites its members to join their dreams to the corporate vision of the group. The assumption here is that both the community and the individual have a dream. The balance between the individual and the corporate dream is most important. A faith community is not a neutral zone in which individuals pursue their separate vocations. Nor does a community provide vocations for individuals who would otherwise be directionless. Recognizing that the Spirit is alive in all believers, exciting them to life ambitions that contribute to the Kingdom of God, a community of faith invites its members to pursue their vocations as part of the community's larger dream and purpose. Further, a community offers models of many specific ways to follow a Christian vocation. It displays—in its liturgies and program for social justice, in the lives of its talented and concerned members—the Christian dream at work. The individual is invited to let his dream, her vocation, grow within and contribute to this community's hopes.

The community's corporate vocation is also challenged and changed by individual dreams. Every human vocation—and this includes each individual and community in the church—remains in need of purification. The purification of a community's dream may begin as new dreams arise among individuals in the group. Members of a parish staff imagine new forms of collaborative ministry; board members of a Catholic hospital begin to envision more effective ways of serving the very poor; women in our communities dream of priestly ministry. Such dreams are often threatening because they challenge the adequacy and stability of the group's current vision. Because it is likely to disturb our accustomed ways of experiencing our faith, we may judge a new dream to be a mere illusion, a passing enthusiasm that will soon disappear. Yet we know from our history as a religious people that new dreams have been part of the important movements of growth and renewal among us. New dreams can break open collective hopes that have become too rigid; they can challenge ambitions that have grown too safe and short-sighted. Our religious heritage has been profoundly affected by individual dreams breaking into and altering our collective sense of purpose. We think of Francis of Assisi, Catherine of Siena, Ignatius of Loyola. But this same dynamic also happens in more ordinary ways in our faith communities today. If it is confusing, it is also to be expected. The collective dream of a community must support and challenge the growth of individual vocations, just as these individual dreams contribute to and, at times, challenge the community's dream. And both dreams, individual and corporate, must remain open to the enlivening critique and purification provided by God's continuing revelation of us to ourselves.

A community's dream also shares the vicissitudes and fragility of individual vocations. A group's vision grows and matures, but it can also wither and be lost. A community may abandon its dream, just as individual believers may allow their own religious hopes to die. When this happens in a parish, Sunday liturgies and special collections may continue, but the vision is gone. Members are exhorted rhetorically to follow the Gospel, but there is no longer any excitement or ambition to transform the world in the direction of the values of Christ.

As a faith community loses its vision, personal vocations wither. In the absence of a strong sense of corporate calling, without attractive examples of the Christian dream being lived out, individuals turn to other life ambitions. As a result, Christian values of love and justice penetrate the fabric of their daily lives less powerfully.

If a community can lose its dream, it can also allow it to narrow into a rigid and compulsive vision. This happens when a community seizes one aspect of Christian life (for example, personal piety or liturgical renewal or political action) and gives it exclusive and obsessive attention. In one group, then, being "born again" becomes the only acceptable credential of Christian holiness. Another, in its enthusiasm for protecting unborn children, neglects other concerns of Christian justice and mercy. Among others, the sense that the church must "take a stand" on a politically sensitive issue closes them to the challenges or alternative insights of other Christians. Each of these dreams attempts to simplify the complex vision of Christian life. But doing so can easily lead to a kind of idolatry: this partial vision is identified with God's will for everyone. A single action or conviction establishes one's orthodoxy and goodness. Antagonistic defense of "our vision" replaces a broader and more open pursuit of the elusive Kingdom of God. A community's dream, like that of an individual, can become a tyranny. Like any tyranny or compulsion, such a dream is recognized by its rigidity and lack of freedom. Defending its narrowed vision of "what we must do to be saved," it tends to neglect its own need for continual purification.

The shared dream of a parish or school or religious congregation is, thus, very much like a personal vocation. Fragile and in need of purification, the group's dream is continually being revealed to it. And like an individual vocation, a Christian community's dream is imbedded in a larger vision and hope: the dream of the Kingdom of God.

The Dream of the Kingdom of God

The vocations of Jews and Christians are rooted in an inherited dream, formed by a vision that has been maturing for three thousand years and more. Abraham sensed that he was being invited to leave his ancestors' home in search of a new land and a different way of life. In his dream of this different future, our own religious ambitions were born. Hundreds of years later his descendants, having escaped from Egypt and now wandering in the Sinai Desert, would remember this dream of Abraham. Was it not the same God who had called Abraham to his search who now impelled them to the dream of a secure and prosperous homeland? In the aridity of the desert this dream took the shape of "a land rich and broad, a land where milk and honey flows" (Exodus 3:8).

This dream of a land flowing with milk and honey seemed, at first, to be realized in the new land of Israel and the kingdom that David and Solomon ruled. But as social injustice and the abuse of power grew, as Israel's infidelities to Yahweh multiplied, it became clear that their collective dream was far from realized. It began to seem to some that the very greatness of their kings and the splendor of their state were distractions from this dream.

As Israel matured (through failure, conversion, and more failure—the usual path of maturity), prophets appeared to re-excite the people in their collective dream and to further nuance this hope. Isaiah and Jeremiah were especially insistent that this dream of an idyllic place "flowing with milk and honey" also include concern for the poor, the widowed, and even the stranger. Isaiah envisioned a society in which ritual sacrifices are replaced by care and justice:

> Take your wrongdoings out of my sight.
> Cease to do evil. Learn to do good.
> Search for justice, help the oppressed,
> Be just to the orphan, plead for the widow.
> (Isaiah 1:16–17)

In such a transformed society, people "will hammer their swords into plowshares, their spears into sickles. Nations will not lift sword against nation, there will be no more training for war" (2:4).

But the challenges of the early prophets and the new dreams of Isaiah and Jeremiah went largely unheeded in Israel. Jerusalem was overrun by its enemies, and the Israelites were led into exile, their dreams shattered. In the second part of the book of Isaiah, written during this period of captivity, a new and powerful dream is imagined: the vision of a servant of Yahweh, a savior who will heal and restore their freedom. The second part of Isaiah invites these exiles to dream again:

> Here is my servant whom I uphold,
> My chosen one in whom my soul delights.
> I have endowed him with my spirit
> That he may bring true justice to the nations.
> (42:1)

The dream, begun in Abraham's ambition to find a new home and revived in the early Israelites' vision of a land flowing with milk and honey, was undergoing a powerful transformation. This collective hope could not be simply identified with a national state, nor could it exclude the poor or the foreigner. In their experience of the Exile, the Israelites were again forced to revise, to re-envision their shared dream. Would this future place of justice and love be more interior than exterior, a realm founded more on personal commitment than on territorial sovereignty?

In the New Testament, Jesus sees his own life as committed to this dream of the Kingdom of God. His ministry begins with the announcement that "'the kingdom of God is at hand'" (Mark 1:15). The urgency of personal change and conversion, so central to Jesus' concerns in the Gospels, arises from the imminence of this kingdom.

If there is great ambiguity in the New Testament about the Kingdom of God—Is it to happen only with the end of the world, or is it already occurring in our lives?—we can see that Jesus' life and the Gospels are centrally concerned with the realization of this shared dream. When the followers of John the Baptist inquire if Jesus is the Messiah, the dreamed-of one, Jesus tells them to report to John what they have seen. "The blind see again, the lame walk, lepers are cleansed, and the deaf hear, the dead are raised to life, the Good News is proclaimed to the poor" (Luke 7:22). These personal and social changes are signs of the Kingdom; this is how we can recognize the realization of the dream in our own lives.

Toward the close of Matthew's Gospel we find Jesus telling his followers what actions will bring them into this Kingdom. "'I was hungry and you gave me food; I was thirsty and you gave me drink; I was a stranger and you made me welcome; naked and you clothed me, sick and you visited me, in prison and you came to see me . . .'" (25:35–36). These actions of justice and love, of caring for "'one of the least of the brethren,'" bring a person into the dreamed-of and hoped-for Kingdom of God. In these Gospel accounts of the Kingdom, it is made clear that our own actions contribute to or frustrate the coming of God's Kingdom.

The whole of the Gospels may be seen as an account of Jesus joining his own life ambition to the dream of the Kingdom. His own actions—compassionately healing some while accusing others of falseness and injustice; his intense involvement with others alternating with periods of retreat and quiet—are guided by a vision of a certain style of life. Concern for healing and personal change overshadowed an interest in a strict observance of the many laws of Jewish life. And life clearly had an urgency about it: God's Kingdom is about to be realized, and we must change our lives, now, to fit God's ambition.

Despite his understanding of and enthusiasm for this dream of the Kingdom, Jesus was himself surprised and even confused by its development. Though he came to Jerusalem sensing danger, it was only in the Garden of Olives that he saw how radically different God's plans were for him. Facing his own death, Jesus had to confront the frustration and failure of his life ambition and dream. His vision of many more years of healing and challenge, of strengthening his friends in this new way of life—this dream was being broken. His own dream for his life was being purified and revised by his Father. Quite naturally, he resisted. He struggled against his death and the shattering of his dream of how the Kingdom was to be pursued. Yet in the end he came to trust the movement of his Father's dream, and he came to see that the dream he had been nourishing and following did not belong to him. His own life and ambition belonged, finally, to the larger dream of the Kingdom of God, a dream always being realized in strange and surprising ways.

In Jesus' death, his earlier life ambition was lost. And in this loss and death, a new vision and dream began to live. The particular dream that would in time be called "Christian" began to grow. Its peculiarity is its convictions (reinforced in the personal experience of believers) that our dreams and careers and vocations are not our own and that it is by dying that they come to life. Christians understand their own life ambitions and visions as gifts, as more than their own possessions. Neither owning nor fully controlling our life, we expect them to be changed, in unplanned and even painful ways, as we mature. The cross stands at the center of Christian faith and Christian dreaming—not out of morbidity but out of the realization that this is how we grow. Vocations and dreams rigidly adhered to become idols; ambitions too strongly defended, made invulnerable, are not Christian. Christian dreams, named for the person who most powerfully shapes our dreaming, expectably change as they are purified and come to match the dream that God is dreaming for us all.

The Story of Three Dreams

A Christian vocation may be described as a dream, God's dream for my life, developing in my imagination. Such a dream is gradually revealed to us in the various achievements and reversals of adult life. Because it is sometimes fragile, a personal vocation may be neglected and then wither. Or it may become compulsive and too well defended. Christian ministry always entails a fostering of dreams: clarifying and purifying our vocations, we come closer to imagining what God is about in our life.

These personal dreams are imbedded in two levels of social life. They are rooted in the immediate contexts of our families and faith communities. And these groups have their own vocations, similarly frail but exciting. Christian maturing requires the interaction of dreams—our personal hopes in dialog and in tension with our community's dreams and goals.

Both our individual vocations and our community's dreams are imbedded in the inherited hope for the Kingdom of God. This ancient dream is both the beginning and end of Christian vocations. In Abraham's dream our vocations began; our best ambitions seek to make the Kingdom come true. About any individual or community vocation we may ask, What does it have to do with the Kingdom of God? Here we find the standard against which we judge the value of our dreams.

Christian maturing is thus an interplay of three dreams. In the mutual jostling, critique, and support of these three dreams, we continue to uncover the purpose and possibility of our Christian life. Here too we see anew the place of the church itself. No longer sensing itself the proud possessor of God's unambiguous plan for humankind, the church guards a fragile and partial vision of God's dream for us. As a church we have yet to imagine what God has in store for us. If this humbles us as an institution, it can also excite us: we are in the midst of a revelation. All the dreams have not been dreamed; the church's vocation is still being revealed.

In his life, Jesus both proclaimed the coming of the Kingdom and announced its location: "'The Kingdom of God is within you'" (Luke 17:21). We might still ask, Where is it within us? The answer may be that it is in our imagination. The dream of the Kingdom of God is real because it already exists in us. It is frail and in need of nurturance because it exists mostly in our imagination. This dream of God is not simply beyond us; if it were, we could not even imagine it. It is within us, and not just in an individualistic fashion. The "you" of the New Testament statement is plural: the Kingdom of God is stirring in our shared visions, in our community's ambitions and hopes. This is good news for communities of faith. Surviving the clash of different hopes and visions, we can still generate in our shared life that ancient dream of the Kingdom of God. Pursuing our vocations, personal and corporate, we move this dream of God closer to its realization.

Reflective Exercises

Trace the maturing of your own dream and vocation by asking the following questions:
1. When did I first become aware of my ambition for my life? (Take time to return in your memory to explore the early shape of this dream.)
2. How have my best hopes for my life mellowed and changed over the past decade?
3. What is the most significant crisis that my dream and vocation have undergone? How was my dream threatened, wounded, or purified in that crisis?

It may also be fruitful to explore the connections between your personal vocation and the social dreams that influence it.

1. What are the dreams or deepest hopes of the group that is most important in my life? (This may be your family or workplace or religious congregation.)
2. How does this corporate dream support or challenge my own vocation?

 3

A Vocation Develops:
Child to Disciple

Child of God, disciple of the Lord, steward of the faith—these are enduring images of Christian spirituality. Each of these images, rooted in sacred Scripture and richly elaborated in Christian piety, has helped shape the awareness of a Christian vocation. Taken alone, each celebrates a central religious conviction. Taken together, they suggest a pattern of spiritual development that gives shape to Christian maturing. In this chapter and the next we place these images in a developmental context, linking these movements of growth. The child of God is meant to mature into the disciple without leaving the strengths of childhood behind. The disciple, already in an important early stage of religious adulthood, is being readied for new roles of stewardship in the community of faith. In this more authoritative stage of stewardship, discipleship is not to be abandoned but matured. The image of religious development here is not a staircase of rigid roles but a spiral of widening strengths: the child survives in the disciple, the disciple matures and endures in the steward.

Child of God

We begin our lives, both biologically and religiously, as children. As children we know ourselves to be dependent, necessarily and properly so. We receive life and care from our parents; as Christians we confess a profound and unending dependence on God. This dependence is both a characteristic of childhood and one of its greatest strengths. Our maturing requires the expansion of this dependence as it ripens into the adult strengths of reliance and reliability. But, as we shall see later in this chapter, this expansion is a transformation of dependence rather than its abandonment.

It is in our early experiences of dependence as children that we first learn to trust the power of others. This foundational experience of dependence—of finding strength in others who are reliable in the face of our needs—is the first stage of the lifelong journey toward adult interdependence. Maturity invites us toward a complex dependability: we *become* strong enough for others to depend on us even as we *remain* able to depend on others, to trust their strength, to be vulnerable to those we love.

If dependence is the first characteristic of childhood, a second is playfulness. A child is essentially a player. In the free space of childhood, before the "serious business" of adult life overtakes us, we begin our play. Feeling the delight of our bodies and testing the limits in our environment, we "play" at life. The root of this play is imagination. In childhood, if we are fortunate, the extraordinary power of imagination begins to flex and develop within us. In play we are able to alter our world, to invent new playmates, to name— and in this way begin to befriend—some of the surprising forces arising within us. These two strengths of childhood, dependence and play, are important to maturity as well.

The Paradox of Childhood

Christians experience a peculiar paradox in their ambition to mature. We share the development described by Saint Paul.

> When I was a child I used to talk like a child, and think like a child, and argue like a child, but now I am an adult, *all childish ways are put behind me.* (1 Corinthians 13:11)

These "childish ways" are specified elsewhere in the Pauline letters. The child suffers the severe dependency of the slave (Galatians 4), and the child, without the experience to give it a sure sense of purpose, is necessarily "tossed one way and another and carried along by every wind of doctrine, at the mercy of all the tricks men play and their cleverness in practicing deceit" (Ephesians 4:14).

Yet we know that childhood is not to be too thoroughly abandoned. We remember Jesus' provocative statement that "'unless you change and become like little children, you will never enter the kingdom of heaven'" (Matthew 18:3). A conversion is required for the recovery of childhood demanded in Christian maturing. How are we to outgrow childhood and simultaneously make our return?

We can approach this paradox by noting two temptations in the movement out of childhood: we may fail by leaving behind the strengths first experienced as a child or by refusing to accept the new strengths required of the adult. In the first temptation, the attempt is to escape dependency. In an eagerness to become an independent and able adult, I may shrug off every manner of dependence. I become "my own person," a full individualist. I wrench myself away from "childish" attachments to other people, those ambiguous ties that bind me both in love and control. Especially if I have experienced my childhood dependence as demeaning and manipulative, I am likely to be wary of adult intimacy and its commitments of affection and fidelity. Defensive and cautious about getting too close to others, I try to become strong enough to stand alone. Following this path of "mock maturity," I am also likely to abandon imagination and play. If, as in dependence, I identify these as childish, I must leave them behind in my trek into the gray sobriety of adult life. Thus the American stereotype: an adult who is serious and independent, an earnest achiever who can "go it alone," a "grown-up" in whom the child (and all its delights) has truly died.

But there is an opposite temptation in the movement beyond childhood—to cling to dependence too long. Frightened by the possibility of failure, I am reluctant to move beyond the secure realm where "other people know best." Or, unsure of my own ability, I am unwilling to set out on my own, afraid to test myself in the public realm. These are normal anxieties in the movement beyond adolescence. For some of us, however, the struggle overwhelms. Instead of gradually letting go of these dependencies of childhood, I hold on to them as the best defense against a confusing adult world. Here dependence, originally a childlike grace, becomes childish.

Religiously this is evidenced in the midlife Christian who, while responsible in family and career matters, remains overly dependent in religious affairs. Unable to depend on inner resources (which should, by now, have been tested and seasoned by several decades of adult experience), such an adult acts "like a child" in religious and moral areas.

This path of immaturity does not always result from personal failing alone. It is engendered and reinforced by institutions that have succumbed to the temptation of paternalism. Paternalism, as we shall see in Chapter Twelve, twists the compelling symbol of the family into a model of social control. Paternalism freezes the categories of parent and child: certain of us are seen as "parents" who care for (and control) others who are seen as—and must remain—children. The expectable movement of the child into adulthood, into a position of greater responsibility and authority for his own life, is frustrated or denied. Paternalism needs children; it thrives by enforcing a childish dependence, by requiring that its subjects remain children. Only when Christian institutions resist this temptation of paternalism are they able to support our religious maturing into adult children of God.

The Survival of the Child

The call to turn and become like children invites us to recover the strengths that we may have lost in an early adult pursuit of exaggerated independence. In the face of the North American cultural commitment to independence, "to depend on others" often seems a negative experience. Relying on others is taken as a sign of weakness, a source of shame. But most of us sense the limitations of this cultural embarrassment over needing other people. As children, we may have taken for granted having others in our life on whom we could depend. As adults, we are more sensitive to the significance of such dependable friends. We cherish such relationships as special and rare. And we become more aware of the strength that such dependence requires. To come to trust others, I must allow myself to be vulnerable to them. To accept the gift of your love, I must be strong enough to admit that I need you. As adults we come to know that this kind of openness demands much of us. But its risks are richly rewarded. Our commitments of love and work demand the strength of dependence. The child's ability to depend, matured by the experiences of the twenties and thirties, is transformed as an adult strength. No longer a childish dependence, it remains a resource linked to the child within us.

Similarly, after a decade or more devoted to serious adult achievement, we may begin to rediscover our earlier playfulness. Sometimes this adult play is interpreted as regression; more often it is an expansion of maturity. In adult play we salute the child in us, giving spontaneity and delight a place in our lives again. The responsibilities and duties of adult life can easily banish the child in us, and we feel the effects of this loss. In experiences of play and in new modes of adult dependence, we allow the child to survive and to contribute to our adult lives.

For Christians the survival of the child has religious significance as well. All our lives we remain children of God—dependent on the Creator's love, heirs to the Kingdom of God. Yet the children of God must mature as adult Christians. As adult offspring in the family of God, we develop into active collaborators in family decisions. An early stage of this journey into religious adulthood is experienced in the call to discipleship.

Disciples of the Lord

As we move beyond adolescence into young adult life, we make those choices which signal a new stage of maturity. In our initial commitments of love and work, we manifest our hopes, test our values, and begin to define our adult responsibilities. Religiously, we might describe this first stage of adult maturing as a period of discipleship.

The word *disciple* is so thoroughly a part of Christian rhetoric that its developmental sense is easily lost. We will focus here on several practical characteristics of this stage of maturity. The move into adulthood is marked by its decisions: I choose to pursue this career path; I initiate this relationship; I select this lifestyle for myself. There is often a tentativeness about those choices, but they are, nonetheless, personal choices. To be an adult is to be able to, to have to, make these kinds of decisions.

The inner reality of these decisions is complex. These are movements of personal *choice* experienced as *responses*. I choose a vocation because I *feel called* to it. My love for you is as much a *response* to your loveableness as it is a decision on my part. I move toward a career that seems to *hold promise*. The young adult experiences these early commitments—in vocation, in relationship, in career—as a *mutual pledge*.

To be a disciple is to experience myself as religiously decisive. I must choose to follow Jesus Christ. I *choose* to be a Christian, rather than simply continuing to attend the church of my parents or friends. Here again, the experience of the mutuality of the pledge is important. I am aware that I can choose the Lord only because I have first been chosen. I sense that my adult faith is a gift; my own choice can be made only in response. Some of us experience this movement into religious discipleship in our late teens or early twenties as part of a young adult conversion or vocational choice. But for many, a moratorium intervenes between the child and the disciple. Leaving behind the simplicity and even naiveté of their childlike faith, these young adults do not directly enter a period of discipleship. Their twenties become a time-in-between, a moratorium when they are no longer children but not yet Christian adults. For some, then, it is not until their thirties or later that they decisively involve themselves in the Christian faith. It may be a family crisis that reawakens deeper questions of religious meaning. Or a concern for their children's awareness of religious and moral values. Experiences with the Rite of Christian Initiation of Adults in the parish may lead them to a mature appreciation of religious commitment. Or participation in parish renewal or Cursillo or Marriage Encounter moves them to choose a more adult stance of Christian faith. Whether in the teens or in midlife, discipleship begins in an adult decision to follow Christ.

The disciple is an adult who both initiates and follows. The word *disciple* itself means "learner." The cultural equivalent is an apprentice. In our first jobs, most of us experience ourselves as learners and apprentices. Whether in an agency or a parish, as a plumber or a teacher, there is much that we have to learn "on the job." New to adult responsibilities, we are still learning from those more experienced than we are. This dependence on external authority is proper to young adult life. As beginning ministers or carpenters or nurses, we find ourselves asking, How do we do it around here? For guidance we look to other people's experience and expertise as we struggle to "get it right."

Even in our commitments of intimacy we begin as apprentices. In the first years of marriage many young couples define their relationship from the outside, either imitating other marriages or resisting doing so. Only gradually do they grow into a confident sense of what their own marriage requires. The person who enters a vowed religious life goes through a period of formal apprenticeship in which the titles themselves—candidate, novice, junior—designate the process as one of discipleship. Although we are already capable adults, through our twenties we are still learning how the interplay of society's expectations and our own deepest hopes will shape our careers and vocations. Over the first decades of adult life, our instincts and intuitions continue to mature as they are challenged by new experiences, shaped by our hopes for the future, and expressed in the decisions we make.

In our religious discipleship we apprentice ourselves to Jesus Christ. We take the posture of listeners and learners—to the Scriptures, to the church, to a spiritual guide. The special quality of religious learning that goes on during this time is captured in a word that shares the same root as disciple: *discipline.* The learner's stance has the disciple look outward, toward objective sources of truth that have proven themselves authoritative. External criteria are important. I test myself against these values to see if I can "measure up." I try to match my life and performance to that of worthy models. I attempt to hold my experiences, hopes, and decisions accountable to the values and hopes of Jesus Christ. Thus the disciple is open to influence: I want to be shaped by the power to which I apprentice myself. It is transformation that I seek.

The effect of this transformation is the internalization of these values and hopes; they now become a part of me. Discipleship starts in chosen dependence on an outside authority. But its goal is that I become less dependent on external criteria as my inner resources become more available and more reliable.

The discipline involved in this gradual transformation is a seasoning of instincts. Over many seasons the values of the Gospel slowly shape our sensibilities about love and commitment, about work and success, about power and justice. As I experience this seasoning, I gradually become more confident in acknowledging my insights and intuitions. Now disciplined, they can be followed. The disciple matures as these instincts become increasingly trustworthy. This developing inner resource (described more traditionally as "mature adult conscience") will be a crucial part of the person's future stewardship.

As the locus of personal authority begins to move within, I experience the fruits of discipleship—commitment and fidelity. It is as my inner resources become more reliable that I become capable of adult commitment. I develop the emotional and intellectual strength required to establish and maintain bonds that pledge my future. My fidelity becomes more resilient. Less "scandalized" by the inconsistencies I find in myself and others—and even in the church—I am able to reaffirm the values of love and justice, of reconciliation and peace, that we as a community of faith hold, even when it seems they are present among us more in hope than in truth. I grow flexible enough to be truly faithful, able—in the words of Erik Erikson—"to sustain loyalties freely pledged in spite of the inevitable contradictions of value systems." Such are the strengths the disciple must take into stewardship.

The Role of the Mentor

For many of us, our experience of discipleship includes a relationship with a mentor. A mentor is someone to whom I can apprentice myself—a teacher or supervisor, an older member of the congregation, the principal or pastor in my first ministry. The mentor is not a parent but a more experienced adult who fosters my growth into adult competence. Mature mentoring—an instance of nonmanipulative adult care—can heal our adolescent biases against dependency and authority. We find we can rely on others in an adult way that is not demeaning. The authority of the mentor is not an authority over me but an authority that urges me to believe more in myself.

The process of discipleship can be frustrated when a mentor is lacking. With no particular person to encourage and challenge me, "following Christ" can become too private a journey—an experience without practical accountability. Ministry to those in discipleship in our parishes and communities will mean, among other things, providing such mature mentors.

The New Testament shows us Jesus in the role of mentor. Mark's Gospel (6:7–13) reports Jesus' words to his disciples as he sends them out to preach and heal. His instructions give hints of what is required of discipleship today. Jesus tells his followers to travel light, to go with a companion, and to be ready to move on.

To travel light is to resist the cultural baggage, the accumulated expectations of adult life. "Light" also suggests less seriousness, less gravity, about what we do. Jesus tells the disciples to travel together. Perhaps this is to remind us that companionship and interdependence mark his followers. This may be counter to some recent images of ministry that seem to demand a self-sufficiency able to "go it alone," the kind of person who is available to give but never open to receive in return. Such a minister may well travel light but always travels alone. Traveling together witnesses to the communal quality of the life of faith; it also gives us someone to play with along the way.

Finally, Jesus encourages his disciples to be ready to move on, not to overinvest in any one place or effort. We are called to give our best effort to the tasks of ministry but always to be ready to move on. Delivered of a final responsibility, we can be a bit less grim and self-serious in our work. We are, after all, disciples of a master who calls us both to work in the vineyard and to play before him in his sight.

Temptations of Discipleship

If there are temptations characteristic of the child, there are specific temptations for the disciple as well. One of these arises from the very nature of discipleship: the earnestness that is part of being a learner. The disciple, like the apprentice, wants very much to do well. Intensely focused on our task (whether this is success in our career or growth in our spirituality), we are likely to be terrified by the possibility of failure. Error and mistakes appear to us as threats to our life ambition. Many adults report that the self-seriousness of this discipleship period, with its attendant fear of failure, left them unimaginative and without a sense of play. Only later would these childlike resources return, as part of a movement of maturity in midlife.

A second temptation for the disciple arises in the challenge to mature. Secure as an apprentice, I may linger here too long. The learner's role is somewhat safe: I am not the one responsible. Others know better; there is more for me to learn; I am not yet ready to be in charge. I may settle for the shelter of being "only a beginner." But the increased demands that accompany the journey through our thirties and forties call us toward a new stage of religious maturity and a new level of service in the Christian community.

Comfortable as a follower, and grateful for the luxury of having others make the final decisions, the disciple may resist new invitations to leadership and greater responsibility. And again, it is not personal insecurity alone that tempts the disciple to remain in this protected place. There are political advantages to be gained in an image of the church that expects most of its members to remain lifelong in the position of followers.

Discipleship matures in us as our adult experience grows and our work responsibility increases. We find ourselves in more authoritative positions. The question that as disciples we asked—How do we do it around here?—is now addressed to us. We may feel uneasy in the awareness that others now look to us for direction. Yet amid the discomfort, we may also sense that it is time; we are ready for this kind of leadership. Our own continuing discipleship is maturing into a new shape. It will soon demand a new name, that of stewardship.

Reflective Exercises

Consider your own experience of discipleship.
1. Recall the adult choices of faith that have been part of your life:
   - experiences in which you have chosen to follow Christ
   - decisions you have made to live as a Christian
   - choices you have made to participate in the life of the church
2. Explore the shape of your discipleship:
   - How have you been a listener and a learner in faith?
   - Who are your religious mentors, those who have nurtured your movement into adult faith?
   - What are the strengths of your discipleship today?
3. Have you experienced the following temptations of the disciple:
   - becoming overly serious, in danger of losing touch with the child within
   - clinging to the comfort of the learner's role
   - refusing to take up the tasks of stewardship

4

A Vocation Matures:
The Emergence of Stewardship

At once children of God and disciples of the Lord, we continue to "put on Christ," to develop in the ways of Christian adulthood. In this movement of religious maturing, once fragile strengths are transformed into resilient virtues. As our vocations are seasoned, we move toward a new stage of life. Even as we remain followers of Jesus Christ, our discipleship takes new shape. With grace and good fortune, we become stewards.

The transformation of the disciple into the steward happens in diverse and sometimes subtle ways. For many Christians the transition begins in the late thirties or forties. An external event may trigger the change, perhaps a new assignment in ministry or a promotion at work. The triggering event may be within the family, as parents realize that they must decide about their children's religious education. Or the impetus toward stewardship may be more interior: I sense I must begin to take my own religious experience more seriously, or I feel a need to be a more active contributor to the future of this religious congregation.

Whether the impulse is external or internal, the movement toward stewardship is recognized in a surge of responsibility and personal authority. We find we are called to trust ourselves in new and perhaps frightening ways. Formerly we could turn to others to ask, What's the best way to do it? Now, more experienced and in positions of greater responsibility, we realize we must turn more to our inner resources in making important decisions. If we are frightened by this increased responsibility—How do I know I will make the right decision?—we are also consoled by the increasing authority of our own experience, accumulated and tested over several decades. During our years of discipleship we have been learning how to care well for others, how to express both our affection and our anger, how to act justly. We find that we have become more dependable. This increased personal authority and dependability mean that we are now more than followers; we are becoming stewards.

Stewards differ from disciples in sensing the trustworthiness of their inner resources and the reliability of their convictions. The steward, of course, continues to be a disciple: the internal authority continues to be complemented and challenged by the authority of the Scriptures and the church. But the central characteristic of stewardship is the ability to trust the authority of one's own maturing convictions.

This surge of responsibility and authority is matched by a paradoxical realization: as stewards we are responsible for what we do not own. Invited in midlife into more responsible jobs and more authoritative positions, we are reminded that what we care for—children, schools, parishes, the land—we do not ultimately possess. A steward, by definition, is not an owner. When Christian faith takes root in us, we recognize that creation and all its fruits belong to the Lord. Yet adult responsibility calls us to be assertive and decisive in our care for this creation. The challenge is to be caring without controlling, to be decisive without becoming possessive. The temptation we experience here is the one that accompanies any investment: when we care deeply for something we are inclined to try to control it, to possess it. Being a parent can initiate this discipline of stewardship. Gradually, sometimes painfully, parents must come to acknowledge that their children are not, in any final sense, "theirs." They are neither reproductions nor possessions. But it is not only by being a parent that adults are taught the lessons of stewardship. If we are fortunate, we also learn these lessons in our job and projects and other "investments." Midlife maturing—its name is stewardship—entails a continuing purification of our care and decisiveness. We become able to sustain our investment in what we do not possess.

Stewardship in the Scriptures

The paradox of nonpossessive care has a long tradition among Jews and Christians. It is rooted in our most basic relationship with our Creator. The writer of Psalm 39, impressed with the brevity and fragility of human life, expressed this relationship most powerfully: "I am your guest, and only for a time; a nomad like all my ancestors." This sense of belonging in a world that we do not own becomes, in our better moments, our religious sense of identity. This "guest involvement" describes a Christian steward today: parents discover that they are guest parents; a pastor is always a guest pastor. Every adult expression of responsibility and authority is recognized as a guest performance. That we fail at this more often than we succeed only reminds us that stewardship is an extraordinary ideal that demands a severe maturity.

The word *steward* appears in the Gospels only in Luke's account, and then only at two points. The first appearance is the famous parable of the faithful steward (Luke 12). This story highlights three features of a steward: the steward acts as a servant, rather than as an owner or ruler; the main strength of a steward is a combination of wisdom and trustworthiness, an experienced dependability; the context of stewardship is absence—the steward acts in the absence of the master. The second appearance of the steward in Luke is in the story of the unjust steward who, about to be fired, is astute enough to reduce what his master's debtors owe (Luke 16). Again the steward acts with a certain wisdom or astuteness, on his own authority and in the absence of the master.

Saint Paul, in his first letter to the Corinthians, describes the same characteristics of the steward: such a person acts as a servant, is trustworthy, and performs in the absence of the master—"until the Lord comes" (1 Corinthians 4:5).

The role of servant is meant to deprive the steward of independence and possessiveness. The virtue of trustworthiness points to a reliability, an inner authority that has developed "on the job" and on which the steward can depend. The third characteristic is more complex and perhaps frightening: the context of stewardship is absence. The authority of stewards arises both from their trustworthiness and from the absence of their master.

Stewards in Absence

The absence of Jesus Christ, begun in his traumatic death and celebrated in his Ascension, is the context of Christian stewardship. In his death, Jesus absented himself from the community. This abnegation had startling results: it brought the Spirit into our midst in new and stirring ways, and it lured us into more authoritative roles in our shared life. In the presence of Jesus, we had but to follow; we had a leader possessed of God like no other. When the Lord is present, we are all fittingly disciples. In the "generous absence" of Jesus Christ, a space was created, a leadership vacuum generated. Jesus' absence invokes our stewardship.

To be sure, Christ is not gone forever. The Lord is among us, present in the Spirit and in the community gathered in his name. But if we really believe in the second coming—the culmination of human stewardship—we must believe in Christ's absence now. We must learn to honor that absence. Our willingness to become stewards is one of the significant ways in which we honor the Lord's absence.

Developmentally, absence seems to have an important role in every kind of leadership and adult maturing. In our forties—expectably the first full season of stewardship—we come into a new intimacy with absence. Our parents are aging and approaching death. We are likely to have experienced the death of a friend or colleague and to have mourned this kind of loss. Mentors and leaders, once so compelling and directive in our life, are less present. We taste absence in a new way in midlife as we are gradually but surely orphaned. But this loss of parents and mentors creates space for our own authority and leadership. Absence is the empty but fertile soil in which our midlife authority is compelled to grow.

But such absence is frightening, and Christian tradition has been tempted to disguise it. One strategy for avoiding this absence is paternalism. Paternalism substitutes a simplified world of parents and children for the complex adult world of shared responsibility, conflict, and negotiation. A paternalistic church divides its believers rigidly between parents and children. It then provides "paternal" ministers (whether named "father" or not) to preside over a "childlike" laity. The exciting and graceful image of the family is distorted in the static dichotomy of clergy and laity. The laity are guaranteed care; they need never confront the absence of the Lord. But the costs of this care are high.

A new awareness of the adult nature of Christian faith, reawakened in Vatican Council II, has alerted us to the limits of family imagery. In its warmth and intimacy, the metaphor of the family can be used to prolong our childhood. If family is the only image we have of our life together as believers, we can fall victim to the subtle shift from knowing ourselves to be children of God to acting as children toward church leaders. Paternalism improperly fills the gap of Christ's absence. It makes present to us "other Christs" who would parent us in faith. But this strategy, we are coming to see, does not honor absence. Either frightened by absence or fearing its implications (the demand that adult Christians trust their own consciences and act with the authority of stewards), we can let paternalism distract us from this pregnant absence.

Stewards of Our Faith

To be a steward is to be authoritatively involved in the Christian faith. More than a child or a disciple, a steward is responsible for handing on this faith. Special challenges of stewardship are being felt today in two central areas of Christian life: the Scriptures and liturgy. We are all disciples of the Scriptures. Whatever our education or maturity or ministerial role, we continue throughout our lives as learners before this sacred text. Our lives are interpreted by the Scriptures. Ideally, from childhood on we are apprenticed to these texts, learning their imagery, experiencing their complex and profound influence. Disciples of the Scriptures in these ways, we are gradually invited to become stewards of the Scriptures as well. A steward assumes a more authoritative attitude toward the sacred text. Responsible for handing on the faith in our communities, we become—necessarily—interpreters of the Scriptures. We select certain images from the Scriptures for special emphasis, we call attention to the contemporary significance of a biblical story that goes beyond its conventional understanding, we arrange passages in an attempt to hand on their revelation more gracefully. As stewards, then, we stand in that precarious position of being both interpreted by God's Word and interpreting it.

An important example of contemporary stewardship of the Scriptures concerns sexist language. In these sacred texts we find God's people called "the sons of men." The persons of strong faith and remarkable deeds that we find in its stories are most often men. The psalms and prayers seem to imply the believer is always "he." A disciple may wonder at this use of language. A steward, in concert with other trustworthy interpreters, begins to change it. This is, of course, dangerous business, for these are sacred texts that we are altering. Yet the responsibility we experience in ministering to a contemporary world authorizes us to participate in that process of interpretation which has always been a part of handing on God's Word. In every age, Christians have chosen for emphasis the scriptural passages that will influence their lives; the steward is someone who does so with an experienced sense of caution and confidence.

Guided by the Scriptures, we Christians celebrate God's presence in the liturgy. Here too we can trace a maturing of discipleship toward stewardship. As disciples we participate in the church's worship: we attend the liturgy, following the lead of the celebrant. Catholics especially have had a rather severe distinction between disciples and stewards in regard to the Eucharist. The altar railing stood as the clear barrier between the steward who was "saying Mass" and the disciples in attendance. In most of our churches the altar railing is now gone, allowing for greater mobility at the liturgy. Parishioners come up to offer the readings; a variety of ministers distribute communion. With more members of the community sharing in the planning of the Eucharist, liturgical stewardship is expanding. The steward of the liturgy differs from the disciple not in excellence but by the mode of participation. A steward *initiates* the liturgy in some way—in selecting the readings, in planning the music, in giving the homily, in presiding.

Throughout the Catholic church more adult believers are coming forward to complement the traditional, sacramental stewardship of the ordained priest. When a priest is absent, lay leaders in South American parishes celebrate the presence of the Lord in the community. In congregations of women religious, stewards within the community are imaginatively designing communion services and other liturgies in the absence of a more traditional chaplain. Small groups of lay Catholics are celebrating the presence of the Lord in their homes—not in defiance but as an expansion of the parish's liturgical life. In all these instances, as well as in the greater sharing of the planning and presiding at parish worship, Christian liturgical stewardship is blossoming. The changes that this portends in Catholic liturgical practice are great. Without doubt, some efforts to reimagine liturgical stewardship may include excess and immaturity. Growth seems seldom to be achieved without embarrassment and even error along the way. More impressive, however, is the potential maturing of the adult worshipping community as its members come to a more assertive sense of their responsibility and authority regarding this central exercise of the faith.

Stewardship appears in our life as our discipleship leads us toward new responsibilities and greater personal authority. But we do not experience these invitations of religious maturity in a social vacuum. The structures of our families and our churches can foster this religious development or frustrate it. A young woman, the oldest of several children, may be forced into an early role as steward in her family by the untimely death of her parents. A recently ordained priest may be thrust into great pastoral responsibility at an early age. Such premature demands for stewardship sometimes provoke an early maturity. Often, however, they lead to exhaustion. In midlife these early stewards may yearn for an experience as learner and follower, for the leisure of a "lost discipleship."

And the reverse of this premature stewardship is likely to occur as well. A woman religious, matured by several decades of service, is ready for wider diocesan leadership. But the diocese is not ready for her. Its structures do not welcome stewardship in women. Or a midlife layman, eager to contribute to his parish, can find no way to express this ambition and readiness. A narrow interpretation of parish stewardship leaves no room for a shared leadership. The church, as God's handiwork, is meant to foster our religious growth; as human institution, it often imposes barriers to our maturing. An expanded sense of stewardship will require a purification of both ourselves and church structures.

The growth from discipleship into stewardship includes a shifting sense of responsibility to one's religious heritage. The disciple is one who ministers from *within* the Christian tradition, grounded in and shaped by it. The steward is also able to minister *to* the tradition itself. Disciples are still learning about the best of our heritage as a believing people; stewards have matured to the point where they are able to, and need to, care for the worst of religious heritage. As disciples of the church we begin to care for the wounds of the world; as more experienced stewards we must also come to care for the wounds of the church.

Such a stewardship arises from a certain vision of the church. The Christian church, as graced as it is with God's enduring presence, is also the wounded and scarred Body of Christ. Human as well as divine, the church is sometimes sinful, often immature, and in many ways grievously wounded. Some of these wounds are self-inflicted, appearing in the gaps between our high ideals and our halting practice. Who will minister to these wounds in the Body of Christ? Children of God are not strong enough to do so; disciples are not yet sufficiently experienced or hardy for the task. It is the stewards, tested and strengthened by decades of adult Christian living, who are strong enough in faith to take up the task of carefully and patiently binding up the church's wounds. Such a role demands extraordinary maturity and a deep awareness of one's own woundedness. Yet this is the stuff of Christian stewardship.

Just as children of God and disciples experience certain temptations, stewards are typically tempted in particular ways as well. The central danger of this stage of Christian service is possessiveness. Involved in responsible choices and authoritative decisions in the community, stewards may forget they are servants. The community or parish or diocese comes to be seen as "theirs." An arrogant or defensive "I'm in charge here" replaces the more open and responsive posture of the steward. Thus the need for the special discipline of this stage of leadership: to recall, again and again, that our authority is a guest responsibility, a gift to be exercised for a short time in the service of the Lord.

A second threat to the exercise of stewardship is seen in the Christian leader who is unable to let go. Accustomed to leadership and its perquisites, a steward may find it difficult to give these up, to step aside, to hand over leadership to the next generation. Clinging to the status or protection of their authority, such stewards contend that the next generation is not yet ready for leadership. And, of course, from the sagacious position of those of us currently in charge, the next generation is, almost by definition, never ready. Its members do not have our experience or our savvy or our plain good sense. They have not lived our lives. Worst, they are not us. But they are the future. And it is in overcoming this temptation of stewardship, in learning to share with the next generation the control of the world that will be theirs more than ours, that our stewardship makes its richest contribution.

The Interplay of Child, Disciple, Steward

Perhaps the most important feature of this understanding of Christian maturing is the continuing interplay and the survival of all three aspects of our religious life. As we mature into adult discipleship, we ought not leave all of childhood behind. To fully abandon childhood means to lose our ability to be dependent and imaginative and playful as adults. And we know from experience how often this happens. The earnestness with which we pursue our careers and other commitments commonly leaves us competent but unplayful. In becoming "successful" in our adult responsibilities, we may become wary of the interdependence required for adult commitments. How are we to become (in Erik Erikson's phrase) "independent enough to be dependable"? How can we learn to combine an adult sense of responsibility with a playful imagination? These are the challenges we face as disciples.

As we mature into stewardship—whether in regard to our communities or our career or the church—we are reminded that we continue to be disciples. As followers of Jesus Christ, we remain apprenticed for a lifetime. We must always remain learners. We sense the illusion involved in the person who considers himself so learned that he need not listen any longer, so authoritative that he need not learn from anyone else. We recognize here the distortion of a stewardship that severs itself from a continuing discipleship.

Religious maturing involves us in the interplay of child, disciple, and steward. Our earlier reminder bears repeating here: the image that captures this movement best is not that of successive stair steps but of an expanding spiral. The goal of growth into discipleship is not to leave behind the strengths of the child but to enlarge them. The movement into stewardship is not meant to be a repudiation of the strengths of the disciple but an expansion.

One of the intriguing aspects of this interplay is the connection between stewardship and the return of the strengths of the child. Many of us have sensed, in the movements of our own maturing in ministry, the loss of the child along the way. The earnestness of our twenties and thirties left us little time or tolerance for play. Imagination was gradually abandoned in the seriousness of young adulthood. Many in ministry report that it was with the advent of stewardship in their lives—the movement into a more responsible job or the development of a more confident sense of personal authority—that the child surprisingly returned. An important connection between stewardship and the strengths of the child is a comfort with error. Several decades of adult living give us experience with failure. We come to learn that mistakes and errors are unavoidable and do not, in fact, destroy us. This insight not only prepares us to be more tolerant of others but allows the child to return in our own lives. Stewards, like children, can take more risks because they are able to laugh at their mistakes. This freedom seems to release resources of both courage and creativity. The "seriousness" of the disciple is lifted, and we become both more authoritative stewards and more imaginative and childlike.

The second characteristic of childhood—dependence—is also involved in the advent of stewardship. In our young adult years, many of us struggle toward a satisfying independence. We are still busy letting go of a dependency on parents that no longer fits; we may be wary of new dependencies, whether in work or in love. But, as we noted in the last chapter, maturity can make us more "dependable" in both senses of the word. We become reliable, strong enough for others to be able to depend on us. And we become better at depending on others. We have learned that such dependencies need not enslave or belittle us. After the earnest seriousness of our twenties and thirties, the emergence of stewardship may include the surprising recovery of these gifts of the child within us. Now more capable of being both imaginative and faithful followers, we are better able to contribute to shaping the community of faith for the future.

Reflective Exercises

Recall your experience in the community of faith over the past several years, alert for signs of your own movement into stewardship.

The stimulus may have been from the outside—moving into greater responsibility in your work or experiencing new demands as a result of changes in your family.

Or there may have been a more internal source—a decision that forced you to trust your own instincts, or a shift in your sense of yourself as an adult.

Spend some time now with these memories, letting the experience of your own movement in stewardship become alive for you again. Then consider these questions:

1. What strengths have you experienced in your movement into stewardship?
2. What risks have been involved for you in becoming a steward?
3. How is discipleship part of your stewardship today?
4. In what ways does the child survive as part of your own religious maturity?

5

The Seasoning of Senses

Christian maturing is neither exotic nor magical. It takes shape in the critical choices and decisions by which we fashion our lives. I choose to marry this person; I decide to change jobs; I resolve to commit myself to this effort of social reform. A dozen or so major life choices are bound together and expressed in scores of daily judgments. These decisions, over decades, provide a specific pattern to our life, giving it both its uniqueness and its special Christian flavor.

How do we come to these decisions? What guides us toward good and fruitful choices? We know there is more here than clear rational decisions based on objective information. Critical choices entail more than a stiff dose of willpower that "makes" us do the right thing. These choices and decisions depend, finally, on trustworthy instincts, on feelings that have become reliable. We "sense" that this commitment or change is the proper choice. In this chapter we wish to trace the maturing of our senses as they become reliable resources in Christian life.

Emotions, intuitions, instincts—these are disconcerting words for many Christians. Is not religious faith that gift of personal conviction that rescues us from the tumult of feeling? Is not Christian belief a certainty that liberates us from the moods and impulses that sometimes threaten to overturn our lives? We may have learned that faith is an intellectual assent, an act of the mind that does not depend on volatile and changing emotions. Or we may have been taught that moral choice is a movement of willpower: Christians are meant to make hard choices about what they "ought to do" and not be led astray by what they "feel like doing." Often enough, what may start as a healthy hesitance about feelings leads to a less healthy mistrust of them. No longer our friends, our feelings are neglected or suppressed. And when they return, they come to punish.

Part of the Christian renaissance occurring these days is a renewed optimism about human feelings. Affection, anger, consolation, confusion, joy—these are expressions of the human spirit. We are more aware today that these emotions are part of the life of the Spirit as well. With reawakened respect for these powerful resources, Christians today are trying to understand better how our feelings are a part of our maturing into "the fullness of Christ."

In Christian spirituality there is an increasing attention given to discernment, the process by which we come to wise decisions in the important questions in our life. These critical questions—Is it time to leave this job? Should we have another child? What direction does my priesthood take now?—are always matters upon which we must act "before all the facts are in." We decide, often with trepidation, guided by intuition and by a gradually more confident "sense" of how we are to act. At the heart of this discernment is the gradual process that refines our feelings and renders our instincts trustworthy. Graceful Christian living depends on the education of desire. Our hunches become wise in repeated purification; they may even become holy.

Christian liturgical life nurtures this purification. Here our emotions are shaped by prayer and movement, by costume and incense. Thus shaped, they can guide and enhance our celebration of God's presence among us. Liturgy is a school of the senses. In worship we recall Jesus' delight and anger and sorrow. We remember and celebrate his sense of when to confront others, when to heal, when to retreat. And the ritual movement of the liturgy is meant to shape us as well, forming our feelings so that they may display something of the power and nuance of Jesus' emotions.

The "Sense" of Scripture

In an effort to trace the maturing of emotion, we turn to the Scriptures. The language of sense and feeling appears throughout the New Testament. But a deep-seated ambivalence about human feelings permeates Christian awareness. Is it not emotion that sweeps us away in acts of passion and sin? We can note this ambivalence in the English translations that disguise the seasoning of senses revealed in the Gospel accounts.

In the New Testament the Greek word *phronein* means "to sense, to judge, to intuit." In some contexts it means "to be sensible"—to have a somewhat matured sense of how to act. And the same word may mean "to be prudent"—to have a refined sense of what action is proper. This single word, then, suggests changing levels of feeling: from sensation to sensibility to prudence. (In Aristotle's discussion of human virtue, this notion is translated as "practical wisdom.")

In the Latin translation of the New Testament, this suggested pattern of our maturing senses is retained by the use of the word *sapere*. Meaning both "to sense" and "to be sensible," this is also the root of the word *sapientia*, "wisdom." The suggestion is that wisdom is not a purely intellectual virtue but a matter of matured sensibilities. A look at some appearances of this word in the New Testament may give us a better vision of Christian maturing.

This word for "Christian sensibility" occurs in a number of interesting contexts. In the famous story of the ten young women awaiting the bridegroom, we find that five are foolish (not having brought enough oil for their lamps to outlast the tardy arrival of the groom) and that five are "sensible" (Matthew 25). The latter five had the good wit or judgment or prudence to bring some extra oil, just in case.

A stranger use of this term appears in Jesus' commissioning of his disciples. As he sends them out into the world, he encourages them "to be *cunning* as serpents and yet as harmless as doves" (Matthew 10:16). The highly developed instincts of a snake, its cunning, is described by this same word, *phronein.*

We find another surprising use of this term in the story of the dishonest steward (Luke 16). About to be fired by his employer, he makes friends with his employer's debtors by reducing their obligations. His employer goes on to fire him, but with praise for his "astuteness." In a crisis, he had the good sense to act a certain way. Prudent young women, a cunning snake, an astute (if dishonest) steward—each displays a certain developed judgment, a sense of what to do in a special situation.

A much more instructive use of this word occurs in the story of the disciples' reaction to Jesus' decision to go to Jerusalem even if it meant his death (Matthew 16; Mark 8). Jesus has decided that he must go to the capital to confront the authorities; it is time to act. Peter strongly objects to this plan. The two men clearly have very different feelings about what is to be done. Jesus, suddenly angered, utters one of his most emphatic statements: "'Get behind me, Satan. You are an obstacle in my path, because you do not *sense* the things of God, but those of humans'" (Matthew 16:23). Peter's feeling—his instinctive response that Jesus ought not to take the chance of going to Jerusalem, ought not to follow this inner urging which could make him vulnerable to death—is opposed to "feeling the things of God." Peter has followed his feelings and instincts, but the wrong ones. He has responded in a seemingly sensible fashion, but in a way that Jesus finds unholy. In his decision to go to Jerusalem, Jesus is following his own instincts and sense, but it is also "the sense of God," a sense of how he is to act that has been formed by his attentiveness to his father.

This important opposition of feelings, of ways of judging, can be easily lost for the English reader of the Scriptures. In many translations the feeling tone of *phronein* is hidden beneath more cognitive renditions. In the Jerusalem Bible the above phrase in Matthew 16:23 is translated as "the way you *think* is not God's way, but man's." In the Oxford Revised Standard translation, all sensing disappears in "you are not on the side of God, but of men." When we return some "feeling" to this passage, we better recognize Jesus' insistence on "a godly way of sensing" that is quite different from our more ordinary sensibilities. And this may help us as we scrutinize our own difficult decisions. As I come to an important life choice, I examine the feelings and instincts that are leading me to this choice. Does this growing sense of what I should do arise from selfishness or cowardice? Or is it rooted in an attentive listening to God's guidance in my life? An important moment in religious maturity comes in my recognition of the trustworthiness of my feelings. Purified in innumerable trials and errors, my senses have become more reliable. This is the gradually accrued confidence, developed over decades of Christian living, that I can trust my senses because they are of God.

A second passage which distinguishes a mature Christian way of sensing appears at the end of Paul's first letter to the Corinthians. Describing the different stages of religious maturity, Paul turns to the metaphor of human development.

> When I was a child, I used to talk like a child, *feel* like a child and argue like a child, but now I am an adult, all childish ways are put behind me. (13:11)

Again we encounter an opposition of ways of behaving, rooted in ways of feeling. Adult maturity entails the letting go of childish ways of feeling or, more accurately, the transformation of these ways of feeling as they become more trustworthy resources.

Again, a "way of feeling" is disguised in many English translations. Both the Jerusalem Bible and the Oxford Revised Standard translate this phrase as "to *think* like a child." By restoring some "feeling" to this passage, we can recover the early Christian awareness that religious maturity is very much concerned with feelings and sense.

One of Paul's most emphatic statements about Christian feelings appears in his letter to the Romans. Paul makes the famous distinction between those who live according to the flesh and those who live according to the Spirit (8:5). The first "set their minds on the things of the flesh," while the others "set their minds on the things of the Spirit." "Set their minds" is the translation of the Oxford Revised Standard; again the feeling aspect of this personal inclination is disguised beneath cerebral translations of the Greek and Latin. A more faithful translation of this passage might be "set their hearts on" or "attune themselves to" the things of the Spirit.

In these passages in Matthew, First Corinthians, and Romans, we meet a distinction between styles of feeling. Ways of sensing that are worldly, childish, and fleshly are distinguished from ways of feeling that are godly, mature, and spiritual.

Senses Being Seasoned

We find ourselves gifted with a variety of powerful feelings and senses: delight, anger, affection, grief. And we come to see that none of these feelings is found in a pure or simple state. As the anthropologist Lévi-Strauss has observed, human instincts are never "raw"; they are always "cooked"—shaped by one's culture and influenced by one's environment. The values and biases of family and neighborhood and society have, from the beginning of our days, been shaping our feelings and senses. Our ways of reacting—whether in rage or sorrow or affection—are never simply spontaneous. These are carefully, even if often unconsciously, learned from life around us. (If human feelings are never "raw," there are always those in the community whose feelings and senses are not only cooked but marinated, even pickled. Too thoroughly influenced by external forces, such persons have lost much of their spontaneity and liveliness.)

An image that may capture the proper maturing of our feelings and instincts is that of "seasoning." Growing up in a Christian family and participating in the life of a parish, we learn, gradually over many seasons, how Christians respond. We watch the actions of those whom we cherish. We learn their intuitive sense of how Christians treat their own bodies, how they are present to those whom they love. We observe how Christians feel about "others"— the poor, the sexually marginal, those who speak other languages and display different cultural habits. We learn over the years how Christians celebrate, the kind of events that bring this group together, how their minds and hearts and bodies are united in worship.

Christian maturing is the seasoning of instincts. In unconscious as well as conscious ways, our feelings are gradually formed by Christian values and hopes. Christian communities provide both the context and the examples for this formation of feelings. And, of course, as with every human and religious effort, we often fail at this formation. A family or parish may itself be less than Christian in some aspect of its own maturity—displaying an unholy distrust of the body or an outright rejection of others who are mistakenly judged not to be of God's family. The young in such communities are shaped and seasoned in these unchristian ways. Their sensibilities are wounded or warped in ways inimical to Christian values. The challenge of Christian formation and education is to learn to provide the proper seasoning.

This metaphor of seasoning has within it a number of different elements. Obviously, it includes the notion of an external influence: the environment and atmosphere in which we grow up is shaping us. Second, seasoning suggests considerable duration: the shaping of our feelings and senses according to Christian hopes for justice and charity takes many seasons. Our sense of how to respond to different situations is formed over several decades by the values, stories, and convictions that are the milieu of our life. It is only gradually and with many reversals, failures, and confusions that we become seasoned Christians. To be seasoned also suggests being both "familiar with" and "good at." We have been at it sufficiently long to know, intuitively, how to respond; we know now, often without complex or arduous reflection, how we as Christians are to respond to a situation.

To be seasoned as a Christian is to have the values of Jesus Christ seep all the way into us. No longer an external authority or set of rules, these values have been internalized and personalized. They have become us. To describe this transformation of our ways of feeling and sensing is to say that we have been "Christianized." Here the word does not refer to the event of our formal entrance into the church; it refers to the inner shaping of our emotions and judgments.

This process of being seasoned must be ongoing in our lives, because we are never fully and finally matured. But the result of this process is that our instincts become trustworthy. Never infallible, our feelings nonetheless become, in time, reliable. The mature Christian is one whose sense—about when to express anger, about how to show affection, about who is my "neighbor"—can be trusted. Shaped and seasoned by Christian values, our intuition becomes dependable. Our feelings are transformed so that we experience them neither as alien nor as simply unpredictable. They become positive resources in our life, part of an inner authority whose movements we can trust. We mature in our faith life, then, as we learn to consult and trust the authority of our seasoned senses.

Another image to help us appreciate the process by which our feelings mature is that of tempering. This metaphor suggests a powerful substance, such as steel, that requires definite and careful shaping. Our emotions are also energies that await refining. The values and hopes handed on by followers of Jesus Christ act on our feelings and senses to temper them, to give them increased flexibility and strength. Our feelings, uncared for and untempered, are likely to become inflexible and brittle. We speak of a person being ill-tempered. Easy to anger, and not especially sympathetic, such a person displays neither flexibility nor gracefulness. Tempering gives resilience to both blade and emotion. Untempered, both are more likely to break under pressure. Christian formation intends a special tempering of human feelings. The strength of this metaphor may lie in its reminder that our emotions are not to be suppressed or enslaved. They do, however, await a certain maturing, a development that will strengthen rather than weaken them. When our affections can consistently support and enliven our commitments, when our assertiveness encourages and guides our actions for justice, then we experience the strength of emotion that is well tempered.

Such is the special fruit of Christian adulthood. With these inner resources to rely on, we are less susceptible to the worldly forces that would seduce our feelings. Or, in Saint Paul's words, "then we shall not be children any longer, tossed one way and another and carried along by every wind of doctrine, at the mercy of all the tricks men play and their cleverness in practicing deceit" (Ephesians 4:14). Gradually seasoned by the values of Jesus Christ, we come into possession of trustworthy senses. While still failing and at times still fooling ourselves, we can more habitually and more thoroughly trust our responses and intuitions. Thus matured, we become ready for that most important exercise of Christian steward-ship: handing on to the next generation the practical wisdom of how Christians feel and act and believe.

A Community's Sense of Faith

If as Christians we have been apprehensive about the role of the senses in personal maturing, we have been doubly doubtful about the place of feelings in community life. At one level we rightly fear the rule of feeling in a group: memories of Hitler manipulating the emotions of the masses linger in our historical memory. At another level, we are aware of the negative effects of conflict and cliques on a group's stability.

Feelings and emotions can become destructive in group life. But here, as in the life of the individual, we recognize that growth requires not the denial but the maturing of these powerful forces. There must be some parallel process by which a group of Christians, as a group, comes gradually to form and trust its shared feelings and instincts of faith. A group's faith maturation develops as the group purifies and comes to trust its intuitions of how to act. This realiza-tion recalls a theological category with a long and varied history, "the sense of the faithful."

The roots of this notion lie in the conviction that the Spirit dwells within each genuine community of faith. This indwelling shapes the moods and influences the movements of a group of believers. This maturing sense of its faith supports and guides its decisions as a community. One practical exercise of this sense of faith in the earliest communities was their selection of leaders; such a judgment relied on intuitions about the kind and style of leadership they needed. Another exercise of the community's intuitive judgment would be seen in its decisions to send out missionaries, to set aside funds for the poor, to struggle to resolve internal conflicts. These decisions often met some resistance; but the group, seasoned by its memories of Jesus, sensed how it should act.

Just over a century ago, Cardinal John Newman turned to this notion of the sense of the faithful to explain how religious doctrine itself develops and expands. Newman argued that different Christian communities embrace, at a level of feeling or intuition, the deepest beliefs of Christianity. Newman defined this sense of the faithful "as a sort of instinct . . . deep in the bosom of the mystical body." Only over time does the official church recognize and clarify these intuitions in formal teachings. Newman's argument was revolutionary in its insistence that a community is more than a docile recipient of church teaching. This sense or instinct in a community is a source of its active expression of faith; it is the root of the group's maturity and generativity.

Another characteristic of the sense of the faithful, according to Newman, is its role in guarding against error. Mature communities defend against false teaching and unchristian attitudes. It is the maturity of its seasoned sense of faith that allows a community to at once feel that a certain decision or development is wrong. To expand Newman's image of a bodily instinct, the sense of the faithful allows this part of the Body of Christ to sense foreign matter, to recognize the effects of harmful elements that may have gotten into the system. Such a seasoned instinct would recognize and reject both humanistic fads and fundamentalistic biases that attempt to pass as Christian insight.

In Vatican Council II, we find a renewed enthusiasm for this sense of faith expected of Christian communities. The Council's document on the church speaks of a "sense of the faith which characterizes the people as a whole," ensuring accord and fidelity in the faith (see the *Constitution on the Church,* no. 12). And this is more than a passive or simply docile sense. This intuition of belief has three functions:

> It *clings* without fail to the faith
> once delivered to the Saints (Cf. Jude 3),
> *penetrates* it more deeply by
> accurate insights and
> *applies* it more thoroughly to life.
> (No. 12; our emphasis)

If the first verb suggests stability and continuity, the second and third point to development and change. This instinct is the impetus for the deeper insight into our shared life of faith that arises as different communities apply the faith "more thoroughly to life."

This renewed interest in a generative sense of faith abiding in the Christian community continued in the 1980 synod of Catholic bishops, which focused on Christian family life. Participants repeatedly referred to the church's need to listen to the life experience of mature women and men in Christian families in order to learn about the changing face of marriage. The sense of the faithful about Christian marriage in today's world will be revealed in communities of married believers. The fourth resolution of the synod observed that this sense of the faithful "flows from those Christian families in which the sacrament of marriage is realized and revealed as an experience of faith."

The institutional church continues to become more appreciative of what it must learn from the lived faith of mature believers. This appreciation is leading us beyond more rhetorical and pious uses of the phrase "sense of the faithful." We are beginning to acknowledge that such a sense, maturing with different rhythms in different societies and communities, must necessarily be plural and divergent. The ideals of universal agreement and conformity must be complemented by a tolerance for difference and even conflict. Dissent, debate, and divergence in faith—obvious and necessary aspects of the church from its inception—are yet to be fully accepted as parts of this sense of the faithful.

Ministering to a Community's Sense of Faith

A ministry to a community's sense of faith begins in the expectation that this group *has* such a sense. The maturing of a Christian community includes the development of a trustworthy instinct of what its faith is and how, practically, it is to be lived. Such a sense of faith, as more than rhetorical, will express the individuality of this community as well as its oneness with the universal church; it will expectably bring this community into both a deeper unity and a livelier tension with the whole church. Such a particularized sense of faith will also ground a community's identity and vocation.

It helps the community come into a more profound sense of what it is for. Out of this sense of faith is born a community's generative ministry. Recognizing who we are and what our faith is for, we come to sense how we are to act. Our ministry—how we in this group of believers are to care for and challenge the world around us in the name of Jesus Christ—takes its shape and direction from our practical sense of faith.

If the ministry to a community's sense of faith begins in the expectation that it have such a personalized awareness, this ministry proceeds as it forms and clarifies this sense of faith. Because this sense of faith is a kind of collective conscience, it always requires formation. The values of Jesus Christ and the Gospels are brought again and again into this community's life—in its liturgies, its educational efforts, its practical decisions about money and other resources—and allowed to shape its actions.

As the sense of faith of our communities matures over many years, it will need repeated clarification. Using the language of the *Constitution on the Church,* we will have to examine how this community is living out its faith: "clinging" to the faith of its tradition; "penetrating" this faith more deeply and accurately; and "applying" it more thoroughly to the changes in contemporary life.

Continual clarification will also teach a faith community about its role in the larger church. As the community reflects on its own faith, it clarifies how it is in accord with and in tension with the larger church. Thus a community may come to certain convictions about justice that put it in conflict with the official church position on the use of diocesan funds or concerning the ordination of women. As the community examines its convictions, aware that its own insights are always in need of purification, it may also present these convictions as challenges to the diocese and other leadership groups in the church. When communities can do this maturely—that is, with concreteness and patience and without personal attack or ultimatum—they perform a most important part of their own ministry. Such a ministry, that of a local community of faith to the larger church, depends on a community's trust in its sense of faith. As with the individual conscience of a Christian, this collective conscience must not only be formed and purified but also trusted. Maturity, for a community as well as for an individual, includes the ability to follow trustworthy instincts of faith.

A mature community will be able to withstand rejection: its tested sense of identity and vocation can survive conflict and disagreement. It is aware that new insights generated by particular communities will often be rejected by leadership groups in the church—sometimes because they are wrong, sometimes because they are new.

The life of the extra-rational—our feelings, emotions, intuitions—has long disquieted Christians. We are gradually becoming more comfortable with the role of these powerful parts of ourself in our growth in holiness: seasoned senses become reliable guides and lead us toward prudent and wise judgments. We are only beginning to imagine how this same dynamic directs the religious maturing of a group. A community's affections and angers and dreads can be healed and tempered over time by the values of Jesus Christ. This is, in practice, the development of a community's sense of faith. On these fragile but maturing instincts, the future of our shared life depends.

Reflective Exercises

Recall an important decision in your recent past with which you were pleased. Call to memory the reflections, discussions, and hesitations that surrounded that choice. How did you come to a "sense" of what decision to make?

Then reflect on your intuitions about expressing affection for others. How has this sense changed and matured over the past decade? In what ways have you grown more comfortable and confident in your own style of emotional expression? How has this style been seasoned and purified in recent years?

❧ PART TWO ☙

Christian Virtues: Guises and Disguises

Whatever happened to prudence, justice, fortitude, and temperance? Enthusiasm for traditional Christian virtues has waned as believers reevaluate the place of discipline and development in adult maturing. A well-known Christian philosopher has even written a book with the ominous title *After Virtue.*

The root meaning of virtue is power: to mature is to become more powerful. But Christian virtue has worn many different guises—from the martyr's courage in the arena to the contemporary churchgoer's docility in the parish.

New expressions of virtue, previously overlooked or disguised, are appearing in the church today. In Part Two we examine virtue in several of its new faces: the imagination as a virtue; the special strength of self-intimacy; anger as a potential virtue; and the virtuous if arduous passages of maturing for the homosexual Christian. Befriending these new shapes of ancient virtues can empower us all in the pursuit of Christian maturity.

6

Virtue:
The Shape of Christian Power

To mature is to grow in power. This maturing power is displayed in
many ways—in the exuberant adolescent sense of boundless possibility, in the shrewd midlife ability to focus one's strengths to the
best purpose, in the sagacious power of mature age to affirm life in
the face of death's inevitable claims. Maturity, then, is about power.

Virtue is also about power. To be virtuous means to be powerful. Our most ancient convictions have identified certain strengths
to be at the core of Christian living: faith, charity, justice. But many
of us are reluctant to use either "power" or "virtue" to describe our
own lives. Power seems to take us toward coercion and conflict;
virtue evokes images of proper but dull persons. Is it possible for us
to recover the vital connections between adult maturing and
Christian virtue? Can we rescue the ancient notion of virtue to enliv-
en our faith today?

There are two hurdles to be cleared in such a recovery. The
first concerns the word itself. The linguistic root of virtue is *vir*, man.
In its earliest meaning this word referred to the strength of manli-
ness, *virility*. The Chinese word for virtue, *te*, has a similar history.
Both words originated in a more primitive sense of human power-
fulness, a "king of the jungle" meaning of virtue. Both words then
took on increasingly sophisticated nuances of human strength until
they came to denote, one in Christian idiom and the other in
Confucian thought, an ability to contribute effectively to the growth
of a human community. The plasticity of the word itself over its long

past suggests, perhaps, that the Christian notion of virtue can be rescued from its exclusively masculine roots.

Beyond this linguistic hurdle lies a barrier of a more explicitly Christian nature. Christian history is—not surprisingly, but regrettably—a predominantly masculine account. Written by men, it has better remembered the contributions of men. Similarly, its discussions of the ambiguous shape of human power—virtue and its shadowy partner, vice—reflect largely masculine concerns. From the earliest church fathers through medieval theology to contemporary reflection, the Christian analysis of virtue emits a decidedly masculine scent. Those destructive energies that have received the most attention are the vices that traditionally have most afflicted men: pride and aggression. The virtues counseled to combat these tendencies are humility and meekness. But these counsels, addressed to women, often produce weak and passive persons. For women, already socialized to nonassertion and overschooled in meekness, the masculine bias in Christian virtue often serves not to empower but to belittle. For many women, the conversion required of Christian maturity leads them away from a culturally dictated docility toward the virtues of assertiveness and self-care.

The fruit of this masculinization of virtue is being harvested in today's church. Some Christians argue that we should abandon the notion of virtue because it is so warped by male malpractice. But this critique, and the larger feminist challenge in the church today, are themselves signs of virtue being stirred, as we search for a more graceful understanding of Christian maturing. This chapter joins this search for a contemporary meaning for Christian virtue. Such an effort demands a double fidelity, a faithfulness both to the best in our Christian tradition on virtue and to the contemporary experience that insists virtue be recognized as more human than male.

The Faces of Virtue

Reimagining the shape of Christian virtue today is more than an exercise of fantasy. It requires the play of imaginations well versed in the traditional shapes of Christian virtue. Virtue has, over our long past, worn many faces. And at times these guises have served as disguises, one aspect distracting us from other features of Christian power. We will approach a contemporary face of virtue by recalling three earlier guises: the Greek face of virtue; Jesus and personal power; and the stoic guise of virtue.

The Greek Face of Virtue

The earliest followers of Jesus Christ lived in a complex society. They inhabited a Jewish nation controlled by the Roman empire, in which Greek ideas were very influential. When Saint Jerome translated the New Testament into Latin toward the end of the fourth century, he translated Jesus' power in preaching, healing, and exorcising demons as *virtus,* virtue. This formalized the dialog already in progress between Christian notions of power and Greek ideas about virtue.

Three hundred and fifty years before Christ, Aristotle had revised Homeric and tragic views of human virtue to present a single, powerful portrait that would shape Western thinking for two thousand years. For Aristotle, virtues were learned dispositions to feel and to act in particular ways. Humans can gradually learn, through instruction and practice, to act courageously, justly, and wisely. These ways of acting can become, in time, *resident* abilities: they dwell within us as reliable resources. Readily available, these resources are "habitual"—they enable us to act repeatedly and with some ease. Thus the free-floating desires and inclinations of the child can be shaped into responsible strengths, into human virtues. This is the movement of maturity.

And this is not a private or individualistic affair. A person grows in virtue only within a very specific social context. For Aristotle, the community essential for the development of virtue was the city-state. Outside such a free political environment, virtue was not available. Practically, in Aristotle's chauvinistic view, this meant that non-Greeks could not mature in virtue, for they lacked the necessary community—a Greek city-state. Slaves, as nonfree members of these cities, could not become virtuous—though they could learn to be good slaves. Greek women and children, barred from full participation in political life, were likewise incapable of the fully virtuous life. As limiting as Aristotle's understanding of virtue is, his view does express an attitude central to Christian conviction: virtues cannot grow in a vacuum, nor are they cultivated in isolation. Only within a truly human community can we learn the behaviors and practices by which courage and justice and wisdom take root. This social orientation also suggests that virtues are not individual possessions but ways of interacting that bind us to one another.

For Aristotle, virtue held the mean between two opposing vices. Thus courage stands between cowardice (too much fear) and rashness (too little fear). Virtue lives in the middle ground between extremes. This conviction reflected Aristotle's larger vision of the human ideal: harmony and balance.

This ideal of harmony included another element that would have a powerful influence on Christian thinking. For Aristotle, conflict was a flaw that was to be, and could be, eliminated from life. Turning away from earlier Greek sensitivity to the necessity of conflict (recall the stories of Odysseus and Oedipus), Aristotle argued for the ideal of a world of harmony, free of conflict. Thus Aristotle articulated a conviction that would be handed on to later Christian cultures: conflict is incompatible with virtue. In its Greek face, virtue wears a placid look. If it bears lines of strenuous effort, still it shows no wrinkles of doubt and conflict. Christian attitudes toward virtue have repeatedly struggled to relate this cultural view of virtue with a deeper religious conviction: ambiguity and conflict are necessary companions in a life lived under the sign of the cross.

Jesus and Personal Power

Jesus was working his way through a crowded street. As he brushed against many people, he felt himself touched in a special way. In the words of Mark's Gospel, "Immediately aware that power had gone out from him, Jesus turned around in the crowd and said, 'Who touched my clothes?'" (5:30). An ill woman, recognizing his power, had touched him. "If I can touch even his clothes," she said to herself, "I shall be well again." And, indeed, "power had gone out from him" to heal her.

This extraordinary story gives us a glimpse of virtue in Jesus Christ. In the Greek New Testament the word for power here is *dunamis*. Its root survives in the English words *dynamic* and *dynamite*. This *dunamis* is the power of God, God as the power that creates and cares for the world. In the Hebrew Scriptures "power" was a name for Yahweh; this name appears in the New Testament in Matthew's account of Jesus' Ascension into heaven. "You will see the Son of Man seated at the right hand of *the power*" (26:64; emphasis added).

This is what Jesus felt flowing out of him—God's power. The woman's touch tapped this power lodged in Jesus, drawing it out to heal her illness. In the Latin translation of this passage, this power is rendered as *virtus*, virtue. In a very early form then, before theologians would systematize a Christian theory of virtue, we find a story of Jesus' virtue. This portrait of virtue includes several elements. Virtue is power, but it is God's power dwelling in Jesus. This power finds its purpose by moving through Jesus to heal others. Virtue is thus pictured as a relational power: coming from God, it passes through Jesus to heal another. Jesus' virtue is not his possession: it comes from another, and it leaves him to heal others.

John's Gospel emphasizes this relational nature of virtue by its negative grammar: the noun *power (dunamis)* is never used, and the verb *to be powerful* appears only in negative contexts. We read repeatedly that Jesus would not be able to do anything except for the Father (3:2; 5:19; 9:33); Jesus tells his followers they can do nothing without him (15:5). The fourth Gospel argues that we have no power unless we are empowered.

The New Testament, then, changes the face of virtue by recognizing its source: our power comes from God. It goes further in its stress on service. Our own power is meant to go beyond us in exercises of care and healing.

One of the powers most emphasized in Jesus' life and most enjoined upon his followers was the virtue of forgiveness. As Alasdair MacIntyre has observed in his *After Virtue*, it is in the appearance of forgiveness that Christian virtue differs most from Greek virtue.

Forgiveness does not appear in Aristotle's scheme of virtue, where good and evil did not consort with each other. In the Jewish worldview of Jesus and his first followers, evil was not simply to be eschewed by the virtuous person; its force could be changed by being embraced in forgiveness. Jesus did not invent forgiveness, but he refined the shape of this power and announced that it was available to all. We can grow into this extraordinary ability, partly from our effort and partly as gift. And Jesus made this virtue an identifying characteristic of those who would follow him. This new virtue would alter the nature of the community, making it more than a gathering of the virtuous or chosen. Now the sinful and wounded and conflicted would be welcome because the Christian community would be a place of reconciliation.

In Jesus' life, human virtue took a turn even his followers found difficult to accept. Power, he sought to persuade them, comes as a gift from God that we are to develop and then give away in care for others. The virtuous life is best exercised not in an upright observance of the law but in forgiving one another. This kind of Christian power is rarely a companion of harmony but instead moves among the shadows of ambiguity and conflict. Conflict is frequently a friend of virtue, refining and maturing it. We know the poignant ambiguity of our growing strength in the midst of our continued sinfulness. We are forgiven but not yet fully transformed. It is this ambiguity and conflict that in time gives birth to a virtue unknown to Aristotle but central to Christian maturity—the power of patience. Before exploring this special virtue, we will consider another source that has influenced the Christian understanding of virtue.

The Stoic Guise of Virtue

The new vision of human virtue revealed in the life of Jesus Christ was carried by his followers to other countries and cultures. In the following centuries the face of virtue displayed in Jesus' life would encounter, wrestle with, and be altered by other interpretations of human strength. An interpretation that has had a powerful impact on Christian self-understanding is the stoic face of virtue.

Stoicism was a grandchild of Greek thought, its immediate sire being Roman ethical thinking. Departing from Aristotle's insistence that we should do good for the sake of the happiness that it brings, Stoics argued that we are to act virtuously for its own sake. We do good because it is good, apart from any rewarding feelings of delight or satisfaction. The relational character of virtue—the flow of power among individuals in a community—was undermined in two ways. First, the Stoics concentrated on virtue as an interior exercise of will. Moral life is thus internalized; virtue abides *within* the individual. Second, they understood virtue to consist in obedience to one's duty; we do our duty when we conform to that law imbedded in nature. Conformity to a universal law (rather than to the messy compromises demanded of a specific community) became central in Stoic virtue. Doing one's duty whether it feels good or not—this was understood as the Stoic ideal. An intense individualism grows from such an ethic. The moral person is seen as the strong individual, the person unswayed by feelings, sufficient unto himself. This ideal, a person unmoved by the conflicts of communal life and the vicissitudes of changing circumstance, appealed mightily to Christians. Signs of Stoicism's success among us are still evident today: Christians more concerned with personal rectitude than reconciliation in the community; Christians more fascinated by an unchanging universal law than by the problems of a specific community; Christians in pursuit of an interior holiness unrelated to social justice.

Patience in Disguise

Over our history, Christian spirituality has been influenced by many interpretations of human strength. Particular virtues have been celebrated in a variety of guises. A good instance of this is the virtue of patience. We can recognize three faces of patience, the first being its political guise. This is the virtue that is counseled to persons or groups seeking change. Thus women and blacks and the poor are told, "Be patient." Here patience usually equals passivity. The communication is, "We will take care of it. Don't rush us." When this political advice is heeded, the "patient" mumbles that "nothing can be done" and succumbs to impotence and inactivity. A virtue is twisted into weakness for purposes of social control.

A second visage of patience, that of the Stoic, appears at the other extreme. Stoic patience is a tough virtue, able to tolerate a great deal of pain. This "virtue" enables one to surmount feelings of loss or injury. Gritting his teeth, the Stoic keeps going. The Stoic "plays through the pain" with an iron will. In such an exercise of patience the person often denies the feelings that accompany the experience. The death of a child or the loss of a job is endured, survived in a blind sort of way. The person swallows the experience without tasting it. Often such a version of patience ends by frustrating the process of grieving that is so necessary for healthy survival. Denying the loss out of an ideal of dutiful rigor, the Stoic appears patient. But in a deeper sense, it is a defensive lack of "patience" that we see—the refusal to be open, to receive, to be moved.

Between these extremes of passivity and compulsive endurance is the active virtue of patience. The word has gained a deceptively passive connotation from its Latin root—*pati,* "to suffer, to undergo." When we exercise this virtue we do not merely undergo an experience, such as illness or loss, but actively *go through* it.

We are not just passive victims of the crisis; we face it. We can look into it and search out its meaning. This stance differs from both personal passivity and the gritty, Stoic denial of feeling. The virtue of grief, an offspring and heir of the human strength of patience, demands an acceptance of loss. This acceptance comes only with a patient attention to the experience, to both its absurdity and its meaning. Again the shadows of ambiguity and conflict fall over Christian virtue.

In psychological terms, this virtue demands receptive mastery. This is the ability to receive, to allow myself to fully savor an experience—whether of loss or delight. For example, we need to be patient in order to be loved; the passive person cannot really accept another's love, and the Stoic does not need it. Experiences do not just "happen" to us. We actively receive them or deny them. We can become adept at denial, attempting to avoid the often threatening information that comes with being loved or being hurt. Without this strength of receptive mastery, lacking the virtue of patience, we may be unable to "hold still" long enough to attend to what is happening to us. And the virtuous path to solitude is patience, which enables me to taste the limits of social life and to grow more comfortable with my aloneness. Thus my loneliness may be gradually transformed into the mellow strength of being at home with myself. Perhaps the best example of this peculiarly Christian understanding of patience lies in the tradition of martyrdom. The martyrs manifested patience in undergoing suffering and death. But they were more than victims; they were witnesses. "Witness" is the meaning of the word *martyr*; it catches the agency and assertion required for this act. One *performed* martyrdom, chose it, entered it.

The turmoil in the church today seems to call for the exercise of a contemporary expression of patience. We are caught in a complex change, moving from a more hierarchical to a more mutual church, from a more doctrinal to a more experiential sense of faith. Finding ourselves in the midst of this change, we must be patient. We cannot quickly bring it to completion *now,* nor are we able (or wise) simply to deny it. Enveloped in the dynamics of the crisis, we can choose it; we can perform it and witness to it even as we undergo it. Ambiguity and conflict abound: Is this particular decision right? Are we moving too fast or too slowly? Within this doubt and conflict we witness to an ecclesial transformation that is, finally, not of our own doing. This is the stuff of the virtue of patience.

New Cardinal Virtues

The classic definition of the human person portrayed each of us as a "rational animal." We have thus pictured ourselves as composed of the regal power of reason and unruly powers or "passions," such as anger and sexuality. In this hierarchy, reason sought to manage our passions benevolently but coolly. But this hierarchical self-portrait is less convincing today. We have spotted reason as a partner in our worst crimes; we have found our passions to be more friendly than we had suspected. It is not that our powers have deserted us; they are instead busy finding a new way of being together.

This reimagining of our inner resources, only just begun, seems to be moving toward a more democratic community. The inner community is being pictured as a partnership of powers. Reason, dethroned from its privileged position, must find its place among the plebian strengths of sexuality, anger, and imagination.

As this democratic reordering continues, we would suggest that four of our powers merit special attention. These four collaborating energies are a sense of self, the inclinations of intimacy and of assertion, and the power of the imagination. Perhaps we can call these four "cardinal" powers in the original sense of that word: they are powers on which our human and Christian maturing hinges. These are deep dispositions and abiding inclinations. When one or more of these powers is frustrated or warped, maturity suffers.

From one perspective, the maturing of these energies is the subject of this book. In Part One we explored the first power, the sense of self. This is at first a nascent awareness of who we are and what our life is for; this awareness grows more complex as we mature. This power is given special shape by Christian conviction: personal identity becomes located in a history of salvation and in a personal call. This psychological strength becomes the Christian virtue of a vocation when an adult sense of identity matures into a reliable inner purpose that guarantees our life choices and commitments. This religious sense of purpose finds practical expression in skillful life choices. We "do" our vocation in certain decisive leaps, life choices guided by seasoned instincts.

Intimacy names a second cluster of ambitions, urges, and hopes on which hinge adult maturing. This cardinal power leads us to be close to others in affection, cooperation, and even competition. Much more than a polite name for sexual desire, intimacy gives the strength to sustain relationships, to outlast the ambiguities that cloud our attempts to be with others. The power of intimacy would rescue us from isolation and make us fruitful. This native power undergoes special seasoning in a Christian community. Here we learn that intimacy begins at home, in the ability to love ourselves; this is the focus of Chapter Eight and Chapter Ten. The seasoning of this strength into a virtue helps us transform romance into committed love, sexual excitement into sustained devotion. It even finds in struggle and conflict a disguised face of intimacy, a potentially fruitful way to be up close to others. In Chapter Thirteen and Chapter Fourteen we explore new faces of intimacy in contemporary life.

Assertion is a third cardinal inclination and strength. This is the root of our ambition to make something of ourselves, to leave a mark, to contribute. This ambition is seasoned by Christian values into the virtue of assertiveness. The flexing of our assertive power finds its virtuous place between the extremes of passivity and aggression. We consider this personal face of power in Chapter Eleven. An especially troublesome aspect of Christian assertiveness is anger. Is it always sinful? Or is it not a necessary part of a search for justice? We explore the virtue of anger in Chapter Nine.

The interplay of these cardinal virtues becomes clear: a confident sense of self (vocation) supports our efforts to love well (intimacy); it is through personal action (assertion) that we live our vocations, giving practical shape to our love and to our hope.

Finally we come to the fourth cardinal power, imagination. This ambiguous human energy, long suspect in Christian circles as the source of sexual temptations and irrational impulses, is reclaiming its place today among the special strengths by which we mature. A vigorous imagination is especially required in a time of personal or ecclesial crisis: we must be able to envision God's promise and presence; we are invited to picture, in the midst of loss, new hopes and images for the future. We turn to a reflection on the cardinal virtue of imagination in the next chapter.

Reflective Exercises

How are you a powerful person? In what part of your life does this power feel most virtuous? How do you experience yourself as powerful in frightening or destructive ways?

"Patience" can mean many different things. How does this chapter's view of it—as the ability to experience fully the losses and delights of our lives—fit your ability to be patient?

Try to imagine yourself as composed of the powers of a vocation—intimacy, assertion, and imagination. What is your strongest power? Which do you least trust? How do these powers within you get along with one another?

❧ 7 ❧

The Virtue of Imagination

Our discussion of Christian maturing in the first section of this book draws on a variety of images: the leap of a vocation, the seasoning of senses, the maturing of the child of God. We turn now to investigate their source. Where do our religious images come from? How do we know they are really Christian? How is "imagining" part of religious maturity? With these questions we begin to reflect on imagination itself as a strength of Christian adulthood, as a virtue.

When we try to focus our attention on the imagination, we are reminded of Saint Augustine's observation about time: we know what it is until we are asked to explain it. The imagination seems to be, by nature, mercurial. It stands near us until we reach for it. Then, with a wink, it disappears. And in this playful movement and lack of control we learn our first lessons about the imagination.

Cultural Biases Concerning Imagination

Western culture has tended to interpret imagination negatively. This bias can be seen in each of the dominant images used to explain its role. The imagination is judged to be alternately a passive receptacle, an unconscious force, a childish diversion. Traditionally in Western thought, the imagination has been understood chiefly as a passive receptacle for sense impressions. Take, for example, an experience at a circus. As I watch the show, my senses are flooded with sights, scents, and sounds. It is in my imagination that impressions from my various senses are combined into a single picture—of an elephant, for example—and stored as a memory. Long after the circus has left town, my imagination can savor the special combination of shape, feel, and smell that is an elephant.

Western philosophers have stressed this receptive and recombining work of the imagination. And they have been quick to observe that in this labor of reconstructing sense experiences, the imagination is free to tinker and to distort. So we can imagine unicorns and creatures from another planet, portraits that are "untrue" because they go beyond the information of our senses. In this classic understanding, the imagination is by design a passive receptacle. It can be inventive but only on expeditions of distortion and hallucination.

Another influential interpretation locates the imagination in the unconscious. Here imagination is seen as an underworld source of those shocking movements of rage and lust and fear that arise unbidden in our nightmares and daydreams. Because the imagination-as-unconscious seems to delight in "unwholesome" thoughts, its forces are best restrained. In this understanding, then, the best strategy for health and holiness would seem to be suppression. If the imagination insists on lingering in the dark, the prudent response is to keep it there.

A third understanding sees imagination as a strength that belongs, most properly, to childhood. Fantasy, make-believe, and play are fitting activities for the child. But the child must give way to the adult. As surely as work replaces play, rational behavior must supplant the imaginative delights of childhood. Growing up means growing away from the imagination, toward the serious responsibilities of adult life. To be sure, some stay behind. The artist, for example, is excused from this movement of maturity, allowed a sustained childhood as a cultural exception and a consoling reminder of our former lives. The entertainer and the athlete are acceptable as "big children," forgiven their immaturity because they distract us from the monotony of our serious adult labors. And there are certain situations in which even we serious adults may slip back into the imaginative realm of the child. In the love play and baby talk of romance, in recreational sports and other games, we momentarily allow ourselves to act once more as children.

Imagination distorts the real world, entices toward sin, lures us back toward immaturity—this has been the report of our culture's biases. In these guises, imagination has little chance to be recognized as a Christian virtue, as a strength crucial for religious maturing. What could such a power have to do with holiness?

Befriending the Imagination

Recently, however, these biases have begun to be rebalanced. Some of imagination's "distortions" are now recognized as more than just harmful hallucinations. In distorting the way things are, the imagination is able to envision new possibilities—the way things must be. We distort the present evidence of greed, warfare, and selfishness in imagining a society in pursuit of care and justice. These images can function as empty solace, distracting us from the misery around us. But they can also act as catalysts, compelling us to act in ways that transform our fantasies into reality. In short, we have come to recognize imagination as a creative force in personal and social change. When imagination moves beyond the present and the boundaries of the status quo, it often does so in ways that excite our deepest hopes for a better life.

The bias against imagination as an unconscious force is being healed as well. If the imagination dwells in the dark, it also delights in crossing the boundary to play in the light of consciousness. Our nightmares of rage and daydreams of sex not only conceal deep desires; they reveal us to ourselves. In the splendid if arcane language of dreams and symbols, imagination enters the conversation of our lives to tell of sorrows and hopes we have yet to admit.

Beyond the realm of therapy, we are beginning to understand the importance of imagination in more and more areas of life. Prominent scientists report that imagination is central to the process of discovery, an arena we had assumed restricted to cool, dispassionate reason. Educators recognize the importance of imagination if learning is to be more than repetition. Managers in business and industry extol imagination as a tool in effective planning: without a capacity to envision, planning becomes simply "more of the same." Imagination, then, does not always retreat from the light of consciousness—even if it is sometimes skittish or reluctant to appear "on schedule."

With this expanding experience of the imagination, the third cultural bias begins to give way. To identify the imagination with childhood now seems misleading. Western civilization has given us many portraits of the successful rational adult, most of these unimaginably dull because imagination has been excluded. Perhaps imagination is not to be left behind in childhood. Perhaps, instead, it is meant to undergo a subtle maturing, so that it might appear in new guises in adult life. Two of these mature faces of imagination are empathy and foresight. We will examine these adult abilities in greater detail later in this chapter; here we note only the maturity required for each. Empathy, that complex process of identifying with another, is all but impossible for a child. Foresight, so dependent on a disciplined capacity to escape the immediacy of the present, is equally difficult for the young person. Each is an exercise of imagination, an imagination matured.

This cultural awareness of the new faces of imagination has been reinforced by the recent revolution in religious scholarship—the reunderstanding of the Hebrew and Christian Scriptures. Historical research has shown us that these sources we hold as sacred are not individual volumes crafted by single authors. Rather they are collections of stories told and retold, sagas rehashed, histories rewritten. We have set aside an earlier image of revelation which saw God dictating individual words through the intellect of the author. Our Scriptures, instead, are stories sprung from stirred imaginations, as God's people remembered, prophesied, envisioned their relationship with the Lord invisible among them.

With this reinterpretation of divine inspiration and of revelation, we have come to recognize, again, the place of imagination at the center of faith itself. Religious faith is a way of seeing the unseen, a way of imagining the presence of God with us. The imagination of Jews and Christians has been shaped in a certain way. We are gifted to find traces of God's care in odd places—in manna, in burning bushes, even in personal crises and failure. The unbeliever judges "it is *just* your imagination." We know it is our imagination—and more. These "sightings" compel us to act differently. Through them our lives are transformed (if only a bit) in directions of hope and care and justice.

These shifts in our cultural and religious understanding of the imagination encourage us to explore this ambiguous power as a positive force in adult Christian life. What would this human energy look like as a Christian virtue?

The Virtuous Imagination

We have been examining the imagination as a versatile adult strength, a special way that we are powerful. This power ebbs and flows in intriguing ways. It can develop into a reliable and resilient resource; it can wither and grow silent; it can join forces with rebellious or destructive urges within us.

Thus we come to the practical questions: What about the development of the imagination? How does this ambiguous power grow into a Christian virtue? How does it retain its energy and verve as it is influenced by the values and hopes of Jesus Christ? These, then, are the concerns in the seasoning of the imagination: the *shaping* of the imagination (how it becomes virtuous); its *accountability* (how we decide whether it is virtuous); and its *exercise* (how we employ it in virtuous actions). We will use a continuum here to help us illustrate the seasoning of this Christian virtue.

Western tradition has held that "virtue stands in the middle" *(in medio stat virtus).* We may imagine, then, that this power in us acts in virtuous ways as it moves between extremes of undesirable behavior. The virtue of imagination lies on a continuum between the dangers of impotence and compulsion.

A CONTINUUM OF THE IMAGINATION AS AN AMBIGUOUS POWER

Impotence . . . . . . Virtuous Imaginings . . . . . . Compulsion
(Stagnation) (Forcefulness)

The image of a continuum captures the movement and pluralism within the imagination. We experience the imagination differently at different points in our lives. Knowing it as a ready resource for years, I may feel my imagination wither in a time of stagnation or fatigue. At another time, when I am under pressure on some project, I may experience my imagination as compulsive, as a force driving me on in ways that consume both my energy and my peace of mind. The shaping of the imagination involves the wooing of this power toward the middle of the continuum, calling it out from stagnation and rescuing it from compulsion.

While there is movement along the continuum in each of us, we differ from one another in where we most regularly dwell. One person frequently feels the pull toward stagnation; another may be

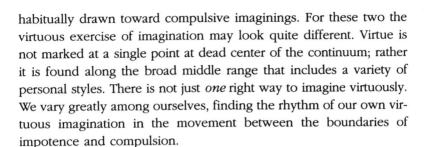

habitually drawn toward compulsive imaginings. For these two the virtuous exercise of imagination may look quite different. Virtue is not marked at a single point at dead center of the continuum; rather it is found along the broad middle range that includes a variety of personal styles. There is not just *one* right way to imagine virtuously. We vary greatly among ourselves, finding the rhythm of our own virtuous imagination in the movement between the boundaries of impotence and compulsion.

Empathy and Foresight

Sometimes we experience the imagination for its own sake in the delight of our reveries and daydreams. But imagination serves us in other important ways as well. The strengths of adult imagination are particularly evident in empathy and foresight. In empathy we cross over to the feeling world of others. Entering into their pain or joy, we experience compassion: we share their "passion" or feeling. Without this capacity for empathy we are each stranded in our own private world.

The effectiveness of our care for others arises less from a clear understanding of "their problems" than from an ability to identify with them in feeling. It is imagination that makes this identification possible. As I listen to the particular details of another person's pain or joy, I may find some of its elements different or even alien from my own experience. I have never been divorced (and so, never known *that* pain); I have never given birth to a child (and so, am ignorant of *that* delight). But as I listen well, these feelings become less alien to me. In nuance they are close to pain I have known, to joy I have savored. Then I am able to share these feelings. It is empathy that enables me to "cross over" into the feelings of another, to sense what they mean in this other person's world. And imagination is the bridge that gives me entry. As my imagination connects me with your world of feeling, I groan or laugh or wince. Each of these responses says, "I have arrived at your feeling; I truly stand with you now."

There are bogus behaviors that mimic empathy but lack its virtuous strength. The first shifts the focus of attention from the other person back to me. I seize upon another's pain or joy and quickly match it with my own. It is such counterfeit empathy that insists,

"I know exactly how you feel" or contends, "If you think you have it bad, just wait 'til I tell you what happened to me!" A second counterfeit response lets me be swallowed up in the other's experience. Fully absorbed in your world, I am overwhelmed by your feelings. But this is not a stance that lets me "stand with" you. My fusion with you does not allow the distinction and distance that empathy demands.

Empathy's special virtue is its ability, grounded in the imagination, to identify deeply with another while remaining oneself. In empathy I bilocate, entering the world of another and staying home at the same time. But it is only in league with a virtuous imagination that I can accomplish this feat. Without such virtue, friendship and collaboration—even mature competition—are impossible.

This partnership of imagination and empathy reaches beyond the interpersonal realm. The Catholic church matures as its corporate imagination is moved by the religious empathy of ecumenism. The ecumenical movement is a bridging exercise, an effort to imagine an underlying kinship stronger than the doctrinal borders erected between denominations and faiths. In this effort of the religious imagination we begin to picture Protestants and Jews, Moslems and Buddhists as "our kind." Old barriers which separated "the faithful" from infidels and distinguished true believers from those "others" are overcome. It remains true that many Christians still "cannot imagine" what ecumenism is about. Yet this imaginative exercise in empathy has begun among us and is gradually healing and uniting the people of God.

As empathy is important for interpersonal life to flourish, foresight is vital for the life of the group. By foresight we mean the ability to envision alternatives. We see this strength in planning. Whether it is a party we are planning, or next Sunday's liturgy, or a large corporate transaction, our effectiveness depends in large measure on our ability to envision alternatives. Sometimes the group seems most imaginative, casting up dozens of alternatives. From this rich assortment we are able to choose an attractive path to pursue. At other times no new alternatives present themselves, or a compulsive pursuit of "the one right way" crowds out other, less conventional options. The planning effort seems to break down. It appears that the collective imagination is not virtuously engaged. When the imagination is present as a virtuous partner, its contributions may take different forms. In one context the group may come to consensus quickly; a single alternative shows us the way. In another setting a jumble of conflicting and overlapping ideas may be needed to spur the planning process. Again we see that the virtue of imagination does not take one shape alone. It displays its strength in many forms.

The Wounded Imagination

The virtue of imagination is a plural strength. There is much diversity in its exercise. But what of the wounded imagination, those movements that take us close to the boundary experiences of impotence and compulsion? At times the imagination seems to atrophy and wither. Frightened by some calamity or despairing of the direction of our lives, we feel locked inside. Imagination no longer serves as a bridge beyond ourselves. We cannot "feel" for others; we no longer seem to care about anything. At such times we are experiencing the imagination as wounded. I may be so preoccupied with myself that I cannot summon the energy or interest to cross over to another's world of feelings. This may be a brief interlude in the midst of personal distress; it can also be a chronic disposition, as in narcissistic individuals habitually absorbed in their own affairs.

Perhaps the most common causes of our imagination's impotence are fear and fatigue. Fear paralyzes us; fatigue wears us down. In either case, imagination deserts us as we "cannot imagine" what to do. We feel we can neither reach out to others nor envision new possibilities on our own. Imagination's impotence is often apparent in a group having difficulty with planning. Unable to imagine alternatives, we are left with repeating the past, doing it the "old way." Sometimes, of course, the old way is a fruitful way, but without imagination we have no choice. Our fatigued or fearful imaginations leave us only one course of action—repetition.

This impotence can affect the capacity to plan for one's own life as well. In despair, a person mourns the present without the ability to imagine a future that is better. Without an alternative that provokes hope, the wounded imagination may see suicide as the only way beyond the present pain. "I cannot imagine any other way out."

A less dramatic face of impotence appears in stagnation. Imagination loses its virtuous vigor as it slips into disinterest and ennui. The imagination is not yet impotent, but life has begun to lose some of its vitality. Repetition and boredom rob us of enthusiasm. We find ourselves buried in unimaginative activities. We lose our sense of play. Routines become ruts. As we settle into them it becomes more difficult to see beyond, to recognize another way to live. Again, we differ greatly here: one person's routine of rich solitude would be another person's stagnation. Virtue demands, as always, finding the rhythms that fit our own vocation and career.

In the life of a religious group a stagnating imagination leads to the rote repetition of prayers and rituals, to a clinging to symbols and rites that once "worked." Unable to imagine new ways to celebrate, a group stagnates. Perhaps bewildered by events around it, it passively awaits deliverance.

As our imaginative life can slide gradually through stagnation toward impotence, it can also accelerate toward compulsion. When this happens, we do not lose the power of imagination but find its force moving toward constraint. The imagination is possessed of a single goal or fear or ambition. When we describe an imagination as "possessed," we suggest that ancient demons can appear in contemporary guise. In my compulsions and obsessions a part of me becomes demonic, consuming my attention and energy. I have to achieve that goal, no matter what! I must do better than that person, than last time, than ever before. In more extreme situations, imagination can cloud all of life with an insistent image: dirty hands that should be washed one more time; a taint of sin that will not be expunged no matter how often one confesses; a conviction that others are conspiring to ruin me. In these experiences the imagination is far from impotent; it acts very powerfully. But its power is possessed. I am swept along, driven by my imagination. It is in this lack of freedom that the demon can be recognized.

These two extremes of the unvirtuous imagination can be displayed in interpersonal relations as well. One person is tempted to withdraw, to hide from contact; and so empathy withers. Another rushes into relationships, but for purposes of control. Manipulation becomes the habitual style of being close. I feign great interest in your concerns, knowing that once you are on my side, I can count on your vote. My apparent empathy disguises a deeper intent—to use you for my purposes. We sense such manipulation in the leader who encourages a group to participate in decision making—imagining new possibilities, brainstorming alternatives—as long as it finally arrives at the decision that the leader already knows to be "right."

Constraining images of the "strong leader," who knows the answer and need not depend on others, block the group's genuine exercise of imagination.

Yet another way the demon of obsession invades the imagination is in giving us *too much* foresight. In facing a decision, we see too many possibilities; multiple options and dangerous consequences flood our imagination. The power to envision is not friendly now, but crippling. The violent assault of these future possibilities may hurl us to the other extreme into impotence and inaction.

The imagination becomes virtuous as its woundedness is healed. This seasoning of the imagination has a double task: to rescue the imagination from impotence and to exorcise it of its compulsions. As Christians, we pursue this healing in the context of our imaginative heritage, the stories and symbols of the Scriptures. The Hebrew and Christian Scriptures are our canon of the imagination, the standard and guide for Christian imagining. Our imagination is seasoned as over many seasons we bring ourselves receptively before the Word of God. In worship and celebration, in reading and prayer, we bathe our imagination in biblical stories and images. These stories are not fossils or dead remains, but lively and enlivening visions. They are images which can heal our impotence, inviting us to hope again, to imagine new ways to live, to forgive, to celebrate the presence of God among us. They are images that exorcise our demons, that drive out our compulsions and liberate our imagination. Healed by such liberating visions, our imagination turns from obsessive control and achievement toward more graceful pursuits of justice and mercy and love.

Shaped by Gospel images, we exercise our imagination always between the perils of impotence and compulsion. Gradually seasoned and purified, the imagination can become a Christian virtue: the power to imagine the presence of God among us; the ability to remember God's saving activity in our past; the extraordinary vision to "see through" the present and catch a glimpse of what God has in imagination for us.

Reflective Exercises

Return to the continuum that appears on page 98. Where does your own experience fall along this span? Spend some time with each of the questions below, drawing on your own examples of the different faces of imagination.

1. What are the situations and settings in which your imagination flourishes? Take time to consider the factors that nourish your imagination.

2. When does your imagination become impotent or stagnant? What circumstances seem to distance you from your personal power?

3. What are the compulsions that tempt your imagination? Are there particular situations or circumstances in which these compulsions have added sway?

What do your responses here have to tell you about the virtue of imagination in your own life? How might this resource become more powerful for you?

8

The Virtue of Self-intimacy

A reflection on the virtue of self-intimacy begins with the realization that we are, each one of us, plural. Each of us is an amalgam of different and even conflicting hopes and fears. We combine within ourselves a variety of ambitions and ideals; there are so many things we would like to be and to do. Accompanying the ambitions and dreams within us are our apprehensions and doubts. Some of these are momentary or occur only in certain situations; others, we find, endure. They accompany us throughout the years of our life.

The pluralism we find within us may remain a scandal and a secret. We have learned that only "crazy" people have conflicting, ambivalent, unresolved elements inside. "Normal" people—most of those we see around us—appear so stable and balanced. My own interior life, with its abrupt surprises, its anxieties and unfinishedness, is embarrassing. Perhaps it is to be suffered, but hardly to be explored or shared even with myself. Self-intimacy is a virtue by which I grow in awareness and acceptance of the *particular* human being I am becoming. It adds to the strength of identity, my sense of clarity and confidence about who I am, a tolerance and affection for this specific person. It is a strength of mature self-love which is the ground for my love of and care for others.

The less we need to keep our plural self a secret, the more alert we are to a crucial task of psychological development and Christian maturing. This is the task of attending to the ongoing revelation of a self that is becoming. Our richly complex selves, created and inhabited by our God, reveal themselves only over time and only to the careful observer. The self-revelation of God, which takes place in nature and in other people—our lovers and enemies alike—also occurs within us. The presence and self-revelation of God in our own particular life lead us beyond narcissism and invite us to religious introspection.

There are two complementary challenges to psychological and religious development in adult life, and in their balance appears maturity. The first has received more attention in the Christian tradition: the challenge to change, to reform, to be converted. We know ourselves to be sinners, selfish, destructive, and untrusting. In our Christian life we are challenged to change, to respond to God's efforts to transform and heal our wounded self. This is the call to *metanoia*—Christian conversion and change of heart. This requires much effort and a kind of "holy intolerance" with who we are. It is important to note the appropriateness of this intolerance, especially at the beginning of adult life. Young adults are often intolerant of others and of themselves as well. Similarly, in the early stages of their new conviction, converts of many kinds are notoriously intolerant of those who do not share their own clear vision. As we saw in Chapter Three, this impatience with imperfection often characterizes the disciple as well.

Yet there comes a period of maturing when such intolerance becomes less holy. Then the other aspect of metanoia is glimpsed: the challenge to be converted to a deeper love and acceptance of ourselves. As we continue to change—to become more virtuous and less selfish, less destructive and untrusting—we are also challenged to come to a more tolerant love of this particular amalgam of strengths and weaknesses that we find ourselves to be. This challenge is essentially an invitation to greater self-intimacy.

The movement of self-intimacy and greater self-love is not a settling into smugness or complacency. It is a call to bring the variety of things that I am into a deeper harmony and integration. It is an invitation to move beyond the useful self-denial of an earlier stage in life, when it was perhaps necessary for me to look away from some ambiguous, humiliating, or confusing parts of myself. As we mature, we seem to be asked—and for Christians this is a religious request—to befriend ourselves. We are invited to a new level of comfort with our own particular and peculiar self and to a more appreciative familiarity with what God is doing with us and despite us.

Befriending Myself as Plural Now

We are, each of us, plural not only over time—through the history of what we have done and who we have been; we are also plural now. This very day I find myself multiple, with enthusiasm for many parts of my life and apprehension about many others. I am, often at once, courageous and afraid, hopeful and despondent. I find that my best efforts of care for others are laced with a variety of motives, accompanied by a range of diverse feelings. And I realize as I mature that this variety of motives and feelings does not necessarily make me bad, but it does make me who I am. This particular combination of abilities and limits, of creativity and stubbornness, is who I am. The challenge of self-intimacy is to better understand this plural self and to better love it.

There is much information available to us about who we are and how we are doing. At times this information takes dramatic form, in an ulcer or a heart attack. Exhaustion and depression may likewise signal an imbalance, a lack of harmony or integration in our life. Psychological and religious maturity entails the ability to attend to both the dramatic and the everyday information available to us. A different kind of discipline, influenced by cultural norms of achievement and self-sufficiency, urges us to push ahead, to keep going and ignore this information. Such a discipline is a form of self-denial in a quite unchristian sense. Its fruit is more often an exhausted and angry achiever than a generous and concerned adult.

Self-intimacy begins in attending to the information from within. As we listen, we learn more about both our limits and our best hopes. I can begin to set aside others' expectations of me and my own idealistic but abstract goals, replacing these with a clearer and more concrete awareness of what my own life offers. I then come into the rhythm of my adulthood and into a greater comfort and patience with my own life journey.

Self-intimacy can result in a clearer sense of my motives. More aware of why I overwork or get angry or depressed, I have a better opportunity to heal these parts of myself—whether this healing entails overcoming or becoming comfortable with them.

The goal of this task of befriending a plural self is "self-possession." Each of us probably knows a few people who are deeply comfortable with who they are. Neither resigned nor overachievers, they are doing well what they can, quietly aware of their own limits and needs. Such people are at ease with themselves. They have found their rhythm; they have, in the deepest sense, come into their vocation. And perhaps best of all, they like themselves.

I may even sense some of this movement in myself. I find, for example, that I can work only *this* hard. I wish I were stronger and could work as long as some others around me, but I cannot—and that is acceptable to me. I acknowledge that this is how I look—not taller, not more attractive or youthful, not with a more commanding presence. I look like this—and it is acceptable, too. Actually, it is better than acceptable; this is who I am and I like it. There are, as well, certain recurring fears and doubts that seem to be me. I once assumed that effort and the years would rid me of them. Now it looks as though they are with me for the duration. So I will make the best of them. I may even come to embrace these inner demons, these once-intolerable weaknesses. Saint Paul may have had something like this in mind with his reference to the thorn in his flesh. Certain weaknesses and peculiarities we cannot shake; they are us. Even God seems content not to remove them. Self-intimacy invites us to be more tolerant of these aspects of who we are.

Finally, self-intimacy allows us to live in the present. Self-acceptance means liking myself now, at this age in my life. With growth in this virtue, I am rescued from a cultural obsession with youth, an obsession which would have me apologize for my present age as I grow older. I am more able to be present to every year of my life. I need not deny or hide my age—because I like who I am now.

The religious insight that supports this call to self-acceptance and love is that we cannot wait until we are perfect to love ourselves. A myth of perfection has injured much Christian effort at religious growth. In the pursuit of perfection we have been allowed to hate ourselves as sinners, imperfect, flawed. When we are surprised by human love, we may think that we are loved only because the other person does not really know us. We are tempted to hide our flaws, pretend to be someone else in order to hold on to this undeserved love. But if we are lucky, we learn that our friend really loves *us*—all of who we are, flaws and all. It may take this lesson to remind us that God loves us as we are. In God's sight we are lovely now; it is not our good works, our achievements, or even our penitence that renders us magically lovely. It is in being loved, to paraphrase Chesterton, that we become lovely. This is true for self-intimacy: I am invited to love myself not in the light of future improvement but now, as I am. More comfortable with both my particularity and my loveliness, I become better at loving others.

Reconciling Myself as Plural over Time

As the journey of our life proceeds, we accumulate a history: we have been many places, lived many roles. The pluralism of this historical self is rarely one of radical or total change. We recognize a continuity in ourselves from child to adolescent to adult. Enduring memories and hopes bind the journey and identify it, in all its stages, as *mine*. We may meet people who represent extremes of personal change or stability. There are some who cut off their roots, trying to disengage themselves from a hated or intolerable past; they may even change their names in a search for a different identity. At the other extreme we meet people who have refused change, who have held rigidly to what they have always been. But most of us live between these extremes. As we continue to change in response to life's demands and invitations, we find ourselves unfolding. We discover unsuspected interests and unanticipated abilities. And we learn the deception of language. A single word—such as *priest* or *wife* or *worker*—has been used to describe me for the past fifteen or thirty years. Yet I find I have played a multitude of roles under that single category; I have understood myself very differently at different points over those years.

My present self, then, is an accumulation of what I have been and what I have done—successes and failures, promises kept and commitments left behind. This personal history abides in me in various states of consciousness and harmony. By midlife, however, I can expect this history to demand some of my attention. About this time many adults find themselves invited to reexamine this history and to integrate certain aspects of it into their lives more explicitly.

This invitation to a reassessment of life may arise in a sudden confrontation with a tender part of the past. I am suddenly reminded of the way my parent—or teacher, or superior, or spouse—has treated me. I am surprised by the anger this recollection generates. Blame joins anger: these people hurt me and are to blame for my troubles now. In this anger there is revealed to me an important part of my past, of myself, that has remained unforgiven. I see a part of my life that is ugly and painful, an unforgiven part of myself that I had kept hidden but now demands attention. Or the sore, unforgiven part of my past may be something that I did to myself. Some mistake or poor choice now reappears; guilt and regret flow again within me. The revelation is the same: this is a part of myself that I have hated or denied or been ashamed of. Now I am invited to be reconciled with it.

There seem to be three options when such uncomfortable information begins to surface in us. We can get busy and try to bury this disturbance from the past. Here the hope is to ignore it. We treat it as a distraction; we repress it (again) and hope it will go away. A second option is to seize, with renewed vigor, the feelings of blame or guilt and give ourselves over to the process of punishment—of my parents, spouse, or myself. This option is to respond to the distress without discerning its opportunity. A third option is to confront the blame or the guilt as an important initial phase of this interior invitation. As we experience these strong feelings about our past, we may eventually experience as well the invitation to forgive. This powerful, negative event really happened and did, in fact, influence my life. But, as I may find, I no longer need to blame my parents or other authorities; I no longer need to carry this guilt about my own behavior in the past. This sore and wounded part of my past—part of myself—I can forgive. I can embrace this part of myself, welcoming it into my present life. This is not an embrace that magically transforms the past; it does not make either the pain or the scar disappear. But this embrace and reconciliation with my past is a kind of exorcism: this part of myself, with its harbored rage and guilt, loses its power over me. As I come, over some time, to forgive this event of my past, I dissolve its destructive power in my life. I no longer have to deny or avoid this part of me. It cannot hurt me as it used to because I have embraced it, welcomed it home, and in so doing, relieved it of its power.

How is such an extraordinary thing possible? Christians have learned of this in the life of Jesus Christ. The possibility of forgiveness is one of the most startling of Christian revelations. When our heart hardens (even against ourselves) and forgiveness seems impossible or intolerable, the Gospel tells us otherwise. Christian revelation tells us we can expect the extraordinary even from ourselves.

And it also proclaims the effect of this powerful act of forgiving: the past can be changed. The notion of fate suggests that what is done is done. Forgiveness contradicts this: it gives us power to change the past and the force of its failures. We can forgive what has been done to us—by parents, by the church, by our spouse, even by ourselves. The past, our personal past, is not as finished as we have been led to believe. It is alive and well, or alive and ailing, in our memories and recollections. At different junctures in life we are invited to explore this lively part of ourselves and to further the continual process of reconciliation and integration that describes our growth in the virtue of self-intimacy.

Reconciliation with a wounded, unforgiven part of our past exorcises its power over us. This important result of reconciliation can be discussed in terms of self-defense and the conservation of energy. Self-defense is not a bad thing. We all need defenses to survive the demands and assaults of life. Yet we often sense that our tendency is to over-defend. As we catch ourselves repeatedly checking our makeup, or straightening our tie, or smoothing our hair, we can recognize the energy that we expend daily in guarding this fragile self. With humor, or curtness, or credentials, we armor ourselves against anticipated assaults, real and imaginary.

As we mature and come to a greater comfort with who we are, we expend less energy on defense. More comfortable with this particular person that I am, with my many limits and strengths, I have less need to defend or prove myself before others. Having learned about my loveliness, foibles and all, from loved ones and from God, I need give less attention and energy to hiding my weaknesses, to showing my best profile and disguising my flaws, physical or spiritual.

This is energy saved, energy conserved and redeemed. Rescuing this energy from the purposes of self-defense, we can invest it in efforts of care and love of others. My partner, my children, my career—all of these consume my energy. Self-intimacy invites us to a more efficient and virtuous use of this personal power. And this is an ironic sign of its genuineness: by careful, loving attention to our own life, we liberate the personal energy formerly given to defense and repression, freeing it for more powerful care for the world beyond ourselves.

Narcissus and Religious Insight

Christians have learned to be squeamish about "looking inside." Such introspection is often felt to be selfish, distracting us from other persons and from our God whom we should serve. Christian distrust of self is rooted in a theology of the Fall, which interprets original sin as a turning in on the self. This theology understands human nature as inclined toward narrow self-absorption; it urges us to learn to avert our gaze. Christian asceticism, in such an understanding, turns our vision away from ourselves—from our bodies, to be sure, but also from our own ambitions and hopes. These hopes are most likely to be selfish. If we are corrupted on the inside, then introspection serves no good religious purpose. Rather it moves toward narcissism. Self-intimacy here is not a virtue but a vice, a form of spiritual self-abuse.

Two questions about such introspection are especially relevant—*how* we inspect ourselves and *what* we expect to see. Narcissus gazed into a pond and saw himself, or thought he did. This watery, insubstantial reflection fascinated him, absorbing his attention. He looked again and again, distracted from other activities.

This same image of gazing into the pond of oneself appears often in the Buddhist religious tradition, but with quite a different meaning. Each person, according to one Buddhist tradition, is like a pond of murky, agitated water. We are called to quiet this turbulence, to discipline our lives until the murkiness settles and the water is clear and still. Then a disciplined look into the water reveals not the individual's image but that of the Buddha nature. Hidden in the depths is not just my private reflection but an identity that unites me with all other living things and, by so doing, tells me who I am. Such introspection leads not to a distracted absorption in myself but to a recognition of who I am and where I belong. Christian introspection, itself undertaken to calm the turbulence that our fears, ambitions, and distractions cause in our life, reveals both our identity and God's presence. My profoundest identity is not my individualistic, isolated self. This identity is—and here Buddhist and Christian mystics would agree—a common identity, a oneness with others in God (or in Buddha). This is a parable and an irony: it is by a disciplined introspection that we can find our community with others. To look within apart from such faith is to come face-to-face with only myself; to look within with faith is to come face-to-face with God. In this recognition, this "enlightenment," sudden or gradual, we are rescued from narcissism because we see both who we are and to whom we belong.

So there are different ways to look within. Narcissism, as a compulsion and a distraction, has me searching repeatedly and desperately for a self. Such a search is not a sign of self-intimacy but proof of its absence. Narcissism is not self-love but an inability to love and to be comfortable with myself. The compulsiveness of narcissistic persons, who must search for "who I am" again and again in the mirror of every new performance and relationship, reminds us of their discomfort with the self. Their busy search signals a dis-ease with the self. Narcissistic introspection arises not from self-esteem but from its opposite.

Christian introspection is guided by a conviction of an inner loveliness and an enduring presence. We may not always experience this presence or our own loveliness, but we believe in it. We look within in response to the invitation to befriend this person so beloved of God. Self-intimacy as a Christian virtue develops over many years of patient, tolerant listening to this plural and unfolding self. I come gradually to better distinguish personal limitations that must be changed from those that must be tolerated and embraced. As I come into a more penetrating awareness of myself, I see not only my limits and incompleteness but my loveliness as well. Perhaps I may even come to a tangible sense of a presence within, a presence that does not distract me from my own identity but encourages me further into it.

Midlife and Mutuality: Where Self-intimacy Grows

Knowledge takes time; the self-knowledge that issues in a deeper respect and tolerance for this particular person who I am takes decades.

In the early years of adult life we have as yet only a modest amount of information about ourselves. Possibilities are many; opportunities, ideals, and dreams of success abound. Others' expectations still tightly wrap our own hopes. Our energy both excites and distracts us. In young adulthood we necessarily spend much time checking external criteria of how we are doing; we look for ways to "prove ourselves," to have someone or something testify to our identity and worth.

Maturing describes the process of "finding ourselves"—coming to awareness of how competent we are at what we do and how limited. This awareness is less and less founded on external criteria or others' approval. As we find ourselves, we realize there is less need to prove ourselves.

What was unavailable to us at twenty-five becomes clearer by forty-five or so: an awareness of strengths we did not earlier suspect; the presence of dreams that previously lay buried under the "shoulds" of others' expectations; the concrete shape of fears only hinted at in our youth. All this suggests that self-intimacy is a virtue that has its special season in midlife.

Self-intimacy is not a private enterprise. Few of us find it effective to retreat to isolation in order to learn about and come to love ourselves. For most of us, community and family are the arenas for this challenge. It is colleagues and coworkers, spouses and children, friends and sometimes even enemies who reflect back to us information about who we are and what we are becoming. We learn that our intimates frequently see parts of us before we do; this is both an exciting and a humiliating aspect of being "up close," whether in work or in love. My partner is thus a vehicle of this self-revelation. This unmasking of myself, performed by those closest to me, reveals me more surely to myself and invites me to a new self-acceptance.

As a virtue, self-intimacy depends on skills for its practical development. Sensing the disturbances or dreams within, we are challenged to take the time to listen; as we listen we need the ability to name our feelings. Courage and skill are required if we are to share this confusing or exciting information with those closest to us. Such skillful listening, naming, and sharing guide the processes of reconciliation and forgiveness that are such an important part of self-intimacy at midlife.

Loneliness and Solitude

We all spend much time alone. However busy we become, we still live "in ourselves," having to contend always with our inner life. Loneliness and solitude describe two very different ways we are with ourselves; each is related to our maturing in self-intimacy.

Loneliness has many connotations. Here we would have this word describe the experience of not being at home with the self. I can be lonely in a crowd as well as when alone. Loneliness occurs when I am alienated from my own resources. Distrustful, frightened, or disgusted by who I am, I cannot be at home with myself. I am uncomfortable with what is inside and need to distract myself; I turn up the music, talk louder, get busy. When we are lonely we find difficulty with recollection or prayer; our aloneness distracts us from ourselves.

Madonna Kolbenschlag discusses envy as characteristic of persons who are not at home with themselves. Lacking confidence in myself, I need to be on the watch for others who may be doing better, looking lovelier, getting ahead. With no trust in the inner criteria of my worth, I am forced to look outside for indications of my identity and value. This gives a new and sadder meaning to the phrase "looking out for myself." Living in such an other-directed fashion, I am prey not only to envy but also to depression. Depression is a serious malaise, a discomfort with who I am. I am dissatisfied with my limits, my shortcomings, my own particularity. Depressed and envious persons wish they were someone else and somewhere else. They are not at home with themselves. Kolbenschlag suggests that envy may be a particular temptation for women.

In classic Christian theology, the deadliest sin is pride and self-assertion. Envy, on the other hand, is the sin of those who fail to assert themselves, who fail to find and to become themselves. The Christian virtue that strengthens us to overcome the sin of envy, as well as the curse of depression and loneliness, is self-intimacy.

Solitude is another experience of being by myself. Its connotations are different than those of loneliness: solitude suggests not an alienation but a mellow quiet—a comfort, perhaps mixed with sadness, in being alone. Another translation of solitude might be "being at home with myself." We began this reflection with the image of ourselves as plural, comprising a variety of abilities, shortcomings, and ambiguities. The home of the self, then, is peopled with many residents. Self-intimacy and solitude suggest a certain domestic tranquillity. The mellowness of solitude reminds us that presence to myself is not always an experience of delight. Self-intimacy entails not a banishment or denial of every failed or incomplete part of myself but an embracing of these aspects. Solitude suggests a deep peacefulness with this particular person that I am. To return to the metaphor of the self as a home, every house is, in part, haunted. We speak of families having skeletons in the closet. So too with my own interior abode. The lonely person, uncomfortable with many inhabitants of the self, tends to stay away from home. In solitude, I become more aware of, and at ease with, the skeletons and unexorcised ghosts of my inner life. This ease contributes, in turn, to a befriending and taming—the integration of my plural self.

The fruit of self-intimacy, experienced in solitude, is the ability to be alone. I do not need to clutter my life with activity and busywork. I can, at times, stop talking and let the noise settle. This is possible because I know that what I will be left with—just myself— is good. There will be not just agitation and guilt and disappointment to contend with, there will also be gentle humor (how strange I am!) and thankfulness (how blessed my life has been!). In periods of solitude—whether enforced, as with illness, or chosen, as in prayer and days of retreat—I can listen more trustingly to the inner voices. And among these many contending sounds I may hear the voice of God blessing me with new dreams and ambitions.

Reflective Exercises

To grasp more concretely the multiplicity of your own sense of self, it may be useful to turn to a chart or picture. Start by drawing a large circle on a sheet of paper. Within the circle, record some of the roles you fill in your family and job and elsewhere. Place close to the center of the circle those roles that are most significant to you; place others at a distance that shows their lesser importance to you.

Then add within the circle the names of three or four things that you do really well or aspects of yourself that you especially like. Finally, place in the circle three or four personal limitations that you know and have come to accept.

Spend some time savoring this picture of yourself. Note which roles you placed closest to the center and which are farther away. Note what you chose to add concerning your strengths and limitations. What does this representation of yourself say to you now?

Now list *outside* the circle those aspects of yourself with which you are most uncomfortable. Consider each in turn: Is it a fault or failing that needs to be overcome? Or is it a genuine part of yourself that needs to be befriended, that asks to be welcomed into the larger circle? Is it, perhaps, even an unadmitted strength?

Reflect on how you might deal with each of these unwanted aspects in ways that contribute to the harmony of your plural self.

ᨏ 9 ᨏ

Anger and Forgiveness

Jesus then went into the temple and drove out all those who were selling and buying there; he upset the tables of the money changers and the chairs of those who were selling pigeons. (Matthew 21:12)

Enraged by misuse of holy space, Jesus expressed his anger in powerful physical action. This story of Jesus overturning tables and pushing people around sits uneasily in a religious tradition which favors the image of Jesus Christ as "meek and humble of heart." Is not anger one of the seven deadly sins? Augustine, describing this volatile emotion, put it succinctly: "Anger grows into hatred." Yet in the midst of this enduring Christian prejudice against anger we continue to recall other testimony: the prophets of Israel raging against injustice; Jesus' anger with hypocrites. And we become more aware, in our own lives, of the ambiguous power of anger. Conflict and enmity are often the result of anger expressed; depression and fatigue are frequently the bitter fruit of anger denied.

Alerted to the special ambiguity of this powerful emotion, we look again to our religious tradition. Perhaps Augustine's words are meant to counsel us that anger grows into hatred not always or inevitably, but when unattended. And we find in the Pauline letter to the Ephesians a distinction often overlooked: "Even if you are angry, you must not sin" (4:27). There are, then, ways to be angry that are not sinful. But this can be stated more strongly. If anger is a vice, vicious in its unchecked expression, can it not also be vicious in its repression? Is there not a way in which this pervasive human

118

experience can be tamed and seasoned so that it serves us reliably in our confrontation with personal and social injustice?

Aristotle was among the first to judge that anger could become a resource for the mature person. Three and a half centuries before Christ, Aristotle introduced the metaphor of "temper" into the discussion of anger. An ill-tempered person is easily aroused to anger; a good-tempered person is angry at the proper things for the right amount of time. Aristotle underscored the importance of this ability to be angry. "Those who are not angry at the things they should be angry at are thought to be fools." Such persons, unable to defend themselves or to challenge injustice around them, are ill-tempered in another sense: they have "lost their temper" not in rage but in a nonvirtuous passivity. In the Aristotelian vision of virtue, we become ill-tempered not only by senseless rages but also in the inability to be aroused. With this human resource unavailable, a person may become untempered—that is, rigid and inflexible.

Thomas Aquinas, translating Aristotle's civic abilities into Christian virtues, focused on the special complexity of the emotion of anger. Anger includes sadness (about an injury or injustice) and hope (that we may correct this situation). Whether our anger is justified or not, these very different movements of sadness and hope come together in our experience. Christianity's deep-seated ambivalence—can anger ever be holy?—is evident in Aquinas's discussion of what the angry person hopes for. Is it vindication or vengeance? Aquinas's Latin *vindicta* is ambivalent: it may mean either of these motives. English translations commonly tip this ambiguity, inherent to the emotion itself, in a negative direction by translating the Latin as "revenge." If anger's ambition is revenge, it can hardly become a Christian virtue. But the challenge of anger lies precisely in naming its arousal and taming its intent. Is it a genuine injury that stimulates my anger, or an imagined slight? If the injustice is real, am I moving toward a rebalancing of the situation or rushing toward a vengeful act? Christian reflection on anger, impressed by the destructive potential of this aspect of human life, has tended to neglect anger's more positive faces. A recognition of the positive possibilities in anger begins with a realization of the ambiguity at its heart.

The findings of recent psychological research can assist our efforts to reimagine the potential of anger as a virtue of Christian maturity. We begin by looking at anger as arousal, as interpretation, and as expression—as a strategy of communication. We explore the sources of anger and its triggers, especially the threat to self-esteem. We conclude our reflection on the virtue of anger in a consideration of forgiveness as its goal and fruit.

Arousal and Interpretation

We know anger to be an ambiguous experience, both personally and socially. For most of us there have been times when the honest expression of anger toward a friend has moved the relationship to a deeper level of trust; there have been other experiences when anger has brought a friendship to an end. We know that anger is often an important part of movements of social reform; we know equally well that anger is the basis of much of the vindictiveness and hostility we see in social life.

Our own mixed feelings are reinforced in our culture's contradictory convictions. If we turn to the experts to learn what to do about our anger, we find those who assure us that "repression is always good." Whether discussed in religious images ("a Christian always turns the other cheek") or in terms of etiquette ("a lady never raises her voice in public"), the suggestion is that anger is not to be expressed and, if possible, not to be experienced. But this is not the only voice we hear. "Repression is always bad" has its champions as well—those who extol the advantages of "getting it out of your system." The case here is often made in psychological terms: Freud's work is cited as demonstrating the detrimental effects of denying one's impulses; emphasis is placed on the therapeutic benefits of "acting out" one's rage.

To be angry describes both a feeling and a way of behaving. Most of us can describe the physical reactions of anger, the ways our bodies respond when we get mad: we become tense, our faces flush or pale, we start to sweat or feel a chill. But the *feeling* of anger involves more than this set of physical reactions; it involves the judgment that these reactions *mean* that I am angry. Research has shown that a similar state of physiological arousal occurs in many emotions. It is often not possible to distinguish fear from anger, for example, or anxiety from anticipation by considering bodily responses alone. Human emotions include interpretation. The feeling of anger involves a state of physiological arousal *and* an interpretation of what this arousal means. As an emotion, then, anger is this complex experience of arousal-and-interpretation. It is not until we determine what this arousal *means* that we know what we are feeling; in that sense, then, we have to "decide" to feel angry.

An example may help. I am waiting in line in a crowded super-market. Balancing my several purchases in my arms (I was in too big a hurry to get a cart), I wait for those in front of me to move through the check-out line. As I wait, I am jostled by the person behind me. Edging forward, I bump the person in front who, in response, gives me a sour look. I am becoming aroused, and the name I give to this feeling is anger. Blaming the check-out person, the rabble around me, and myself (for coming at such a busy time), I name this esca-lating emotion anger.

Later that day, having survived the supermarket, I head out for the football game at a nearby university. As I approach the stadium I fall in with the throng hurrying to the seats. At the stadium itself I find myself jostled and moved along by the large crowd. There are smiles all around, along with cliches about the weather and com-ments about our team's chances for victory. I am aroused, and I like it. Here the jostling and the crush of people, similar to but even worse than at the market, stimulates me. This arousal, interpreted differently, becomes not anger but a delightful anticipation.

As an emotion, then, anger includes both arousal and interpre-tation. And we are becoming more aware of what is involved in the physiological arousal. The underlying physical event in anger, as in other emotional states, is an increase in the levels of adrenaline and noradrenaline in the system. These two hormones can be stimulated by a range of factors: physical exercise or injury; drugs like caffeine and nicotine; psychosocial stresses, such as events that are intrusive or unfamiliar. The effect of these two hormones is to put the system "on alert," whether in the supermarket or football stadium. The adrenal hormones are carried through the sympathetic nervous sys-tem to the organs of the body, shutting off digestion, quickening the heartbeat and breathing, increasing blood pressure. The body is readied for "fight or flight." The mind is also affected. Moderate increases in hormone levels seem to sharpen concentration, while high levels sustained over a long time lead to confusion and exhaus-tion. This kind of arousal, it is important to recall, accompanies *all* emotion—not just anger. And whether this aroused state is named anger or something else depends not only on what is happening in the body but what is going on in the mind—on the *meaning* that we give to the arousal that we feel.

To know what emotion we are feeling we have to explain it to ourselves; we need to give it a name. Our state of arousal must be interpreted before its emotional significance becomes clear. Why do we interpret this arousal as anger in some circumstances but not in others? What goes into the evaluation of anger? We name our arousal anger when this stirring accompanies frustration or humiliation.

Being prevented from gaining something that we want may make us angry. It may be an inanimate object "at fault"—a door that refuses to open or a typewriter that insists on making the same mistake. (Inanimate objects—furniture, machines, cars—also serve as frequent targets of misplaced anger: unwilling to express anger at a friend or the boss, we aim our outrage at an object that will not strike back.) Sometimes another person seems to be the cause of our frustration, standing in the way of our getting what we need or desire. Likely candidates here are those people with whom we share life "up close"—family members and friends, coworkers and colleagues. Or it may be a larger social sense of honesty and justice that is being violated, when we feel we are not being treated fairly. But such frustration, whatever its source, does not automatically result in anger. The experience of being blocked causes arousal; we feel this arousal as anger when we judge that we *deserve* what we are being denied.

Norman Rohrer and S. Philip Sutherland speak of anger at the personal level as "a hedge against humiliation." We are likely to interpret arousal as anger when our self-esteem is under attack. But more is required: to experience anger rather than simply chagrin involves a judgment of responsibility. We are angry when we interpret *someone else* to be to blame, someone who should have acted otherwise. Psychologist Joseph de Rivera stresses how important this assertion of an "ought" is to anger. We are angry when we sense that the responsible party could, and should, have acted otherwise. If those "to blame" really had no alternative (so that "could" does not apply) or had no obligation (so that "should" is not appropriate) then we may well feel aroused by their actions, but we are less likely to name our arousal as anger.

Anger awaits interpretation. In certain contexts we may feel constrained to deny this emotion or to give it a false name. If I am convinced that anger is wrong, or that it would entail loss of control, or that I can do nothing about it, I may well interpret my arousal in other ways: I may settle for the vague "I feel bad today" or decide I am depressed. Or I may assert, bravely, "I feel fine"—though my clenched teeth and flushed face say otherwise. When I refuse to name my experience around frustration and humiliation as anger, I block the process of arousal, interpretation, and expression. Misnaming my arousal, I find it more difficult to choose an effective strategy for expressing my emotion. And often, by not expressing my anger, I frustrate the forgiveness that awaits on the other side of this experience.

Expressing Anger— A Strategy of Communication

Anger is a way of behaving as well as a way of feeling; it involves expression as well as emotion. We have seen that the emotion of anger is not a simple reaction to a physiological stimulus; so, too, angry behavior is not a necessary response to feeling angry. The expression of anger involves a decision to communicate. As I decide that what I am feeling now is anger, I must also decide what I am going to do about this feeling. Hostile behavior, for most adults, is not a reflex response that automatically accompanies angry feelings. I *choose* what I am going to do about the way I feel—whether I will act toward you or toward myself, whether my behavior will be hostile or conciliatory, whether I will choose not to act at all and instead turn my attention in another direction.

Anger, as Carol Tavris reminds us, "is a process, a transaction, a way of communicating." Involving both interpretation and choice, anger is best understood as a social strategy, one of the ways we learn to deal with other people. This strategy is evident in the child's tantrum and the teenager's sulk, but it is also apparent in the concerned adult's demand for better schools or health services for the poor.

My choice of a specific strategy is influenced by my goal. If the goal of my anger is to punish you, I may decide to insult you. But I may decide, on the other hand, that the best punishment is not an overt insult but the withdrawal of my affection. Thus appears the strategy of the "stony silence," or the refusal to cooperate. If my goal is not to injure you but to make the situation better between us, I may judge that punishing you will not heal the situation. Instead I may decide to initiate a problem-solving discussion. How I act on my anger, then, is determined by what I want to accomplish. I may not be completely aware of my goals; I may be acting in ways that in fact produce results that are at odds with what I want. But the expression of anger remains a goal-directed choice and a strategy of communication.

The Roots of Anger

Rohrer and Sutherland, in their valuable book *Facing Anger,* discuss the issues that most frequently generate angry feelings and angry actions. In their analysis, anger is most often a protest against the loss of self-esteem. In our culture, self-esteem is frequently at stake around these central issues:

- *power*—being in control, able to influence other people without being influenced in return
- *self-sufficiency*—refusing to acknowledge feelings of dependency and helplessness
- *personal significance*—having one's sense of worth confirmed by the actions and opinions of others
- *perfection*—seeing oneself as without flaw and incapable of mistakes

When self-esteem is threatened in any of these areas—if I feel someone is trying to control me, or I experience a sense of helplessness, or I lose face before others, or I am forced to acknowledge a mistake—my response may well be one of anger. The discomforts of anger are to be preferred, as it were, to the discomforts of losing my sense of self-worth. Thus anger can sometimes mask another, more threatening, emotion. To help determine if there is another issue involved in my angry feelings, Rohrer and Sutherland suggest a simple test: asking myself what I would be feeling right now if I were not feeling anger. My response will often indicate the area of personal sensitivity—whether this is control, reputation, or helplessness—that my anger is attempting to protect.

This rooting of anger in the loss of self-esteem echoes the analyses of Aristotle and Aquinas. These philosophers located anger in the distress arising from what seems to be an undeserved slight.

"Slight" here translates the Latin word *parvipensio,* which literally means "to think little of," to belittle. Anger is aroused by an experience of diminishment. When we are made little of, our life and our self-worth are lessened. We defend against this threat of extinction with anger. Aristotle, putting it yet more poignantly, judged that another reason for our anger is "being forgotten by others." When we are ignored or forgotten, we cease to exist for others. Against such a diminishment, we resist with anger.

Anger Becomes a Virtue

Anger, as we have seen, is a strategy in interpersonal life, a strategy that involves choice. I may decide to express my anger, or I may choose to give my attention to something else, based on what I hope to accomplish here. It is my goal in this interaction that helps me determine what to do. Sometimes my goal is mainly communication, to let someone know that I am upset; sometimes it is to do what I can to change a situation that I find unacceptable. On other occasions my goal is to stop feeling angry, to move away from this state of physical and mental arousal and turn my gaze elsewhere. These different goals will evoke different strategies.

If my goal is to use my anger to help me take action, I may choose to do what I can to nurture the emotion. I recall the frustrating event; I try to keep alive the memory of the injustice that has been suffered. Group support is especially important in keeping anger available to a task of personal or social change. These other people share my way of seeing things (the interpretive element of anger); as we talk together we confirm the legitimacy of our anger and the rectitude of our cause. We "renew" the energy of our anger. In the group we gain a sense of power that goes beyond what I can do on my own. By providing an arena in which emotion can be acknowledged and then focused toward action, a supportive group can also protect the individual from simply being overwhelmed by the feelings of anger aroused.

But our goal is not always to sustain our angry feelings. There are instances where our intent is rather to move beyond anger— toward negotiation, toward understanding, toward peace. These settings call for a different strategy, with different choices about how our anger shall be expressed. Carol Tavris reminds us that "expressing anger" is not the same as "acting aggressively." I can let you know that I am feeling angry and why, without attacking you either verbally or physically. Psychologist Thomas Gordon distinguishes between "I" messages (this is how I am feeling . . . ; this is what I am going to do . . .) and "you" messages (you are to blame . . . ; you have done this to me . . .). In a situation where emotions—especially negative emotions—run high, "I" messages tend to be a more successful strategy. This way of communicating usually makes it easier for us to give and receive the volatile information often involved in anger.

Expressing anger is frequently necessary; learning how to do so appropriately is a valuable skill of adult maturity. But contrary to some commonsense understandings, the effect of expressing anger or "letting it out" is more often to increase arousal than to dissipate its force. Anger is dissipated when injustice is rectified, when a sense of personal control is reinstated, when self-esteem is restored. Sometimes giving vent to angry feelings can be part of this process, moving me beyond apathy (there is nothing I can do) and self-doubt (I'm probably just getting what I deserve) toward a sense of personal worth and power. Sometimes "talking it through" is useful, especially when the goal is to sustain our anger so that it can motivate us to act. But for most of us, these expressions of anger do not result in "getting it out of our system." Expressing anger often tends to keep it alive. And again, this may or may not be useful, depending on what we hope to achieve.

If our goal is to dissipate anger, then other strategies are required. We experience anger in both mind and body; both mind and body can be used to dispel its force. Our efforts can focus on our state of physical arousal and be aimed at counteracting the "fight or flight" effects of the adrenal hormones. Yoga, meditation, and biofeedback exercises can influence the sympathetic nervous system and lower levels of physiological arousal. Moderate physical exercise can channel energy away from angry behavior. Getting involved in doing something else, especially something that demands our concentration and gives us pleasure, helps to bring our bodies around in ways that change our emotional state as well.

Other strategies for moderating anger focus on the interpretations that are part of the emotion. The feeling of anger, as we have seen, includes both a state of arousal and an interpretation of what this arousal means. A change in interpretation can be as effective in dislodging anger as a change in physiological stress. We each have personal examples of this kind of reinterpretation. Our anger at being kept waiting dissolves when we learn that our companion had a compelling reason for being late. Or we excuse an apparent insult when we recognize the strain under which the other person is living right now. Reappraisal is an effective strategy for lessening anger, when that is our goal. As we become aware of new facts or extenuating circumstances or additional forces at play, we can experience a diminishment of our anger.

Humor is another way of reinterpreting the meaning of events. And, here again, most of us have experienced the way that laughter dissipates our anger. Being able to laugh at ourselves and what happens to us can lessen the impact of the frustrations and reversals that are inevitably a part of life. But humor is a tricky tool; it can trivialize as well as relativize. And many of us have felt the effects of humor used against us in an attempt to make us feel foolish in our anger or to belittle our concern.

Forgiveness in Anger

Forgiveness is another effort to reinterpret the meaning of anger. And it can become the fruit of an anger courageously faced. It enables us to start again, to come to a sense of a new beginning. In forgiving I *choose* not to let the hurt I have experienced get in the way of a relationship. The commonsense adage is "forgive and forget." And while in our experience we know that our efforts to forgive are often helped if we are able to forget, it is important to stress that forgiveness is not the same thing as forgetting. To truly forgive I must know the hurt I have sustained and, with that in mind, choose to respond to you not in terms of the hurt you have given me but in terms of who you are beyond that pain. So the order of the adage is important—forgive . . . and then forget, lest the memory of the pain revive the anger and hostility between us. The social philosopher Hannah Arendt notes that "forgiving is an eminently personal (though not necessarily individual or private) affair in which what was done is forgiven for the sake of *who* did it."

Forgiving involves a decision, but it is not completed in the moment of choice. Forgiveness is a process, the process of gradually allowing the hurt to heal and rebuilding the experience of trust between us. This process of forgiving does not bring us back to where we were. It does not allow us to go on as if nothing has happened. Something *has* happened, something profound. There has been a tear in the fabric of our interwoven lives. Yet we can choose not to be defined by this rupture but instead to incorporate it as part of an ongoing relationship. Our hope is that the hurt we have experienced will not become the pattern, but we sense its contribution of depth and substance to the design.

Forgiveness is not easy—either to extend or to receive. In order to forgive I must experience my anger and face the hurt that is its cause. I must be willing to test my hurt, examining it to see if my interpretation is accurate, if my feelings of anger are justified. If I submit my feelings to this kind of scrutiny, I may find that I am wrong. It may become obvious that I have misjudged another's motives or overreacted to an event. Yet even if my original anger was mistaken, it may still be easier for me to nurse my anger than to consider forgiveness.

The reflection that forgiveness requires is likely to show me ways in which I have contributed to the hurt. There are few situations in which one party is all to blame; most interactions are conjoint, with each participant involved in the pattern that develops. Again, it may be more important to me to see myself as the innocent victim than to risk the self-knowledge that forgiveness demands.

Genuine forgiveness also robs me of my hurt. I can no longer harbor it for later use against you. I must surrender the wound or injustice that may have become a cherished, if bitter, possession. Letting go of this vengeful possession, I lose a painful advantage I had been savoring, but I regain the personal energy that had been required to nourish this hurt. In a sense, forgiveness "evens the score" between us; it undercuts the sense that I have something to hold over you. In forgiving, we start out anew, perhaps humbled (we know how fragile our relationship can be) but hopeful too.

If forgiveness is hard to give, it is difficult to receive as well. To accept your forgiveness I too must revisit the hurt. I must remember what I did and recall the ways in which you were hurt by it. I will have to acknowledge that I was responsible; I may even have to admit that I was wrong. Here again, I may find it easier to deny all this. It is humbling to need to be forgiven. As long as I am in the right, I have no such need. To accept your forgiveness is to confess my guilt—not only to myself but to you as well.

Forgiveness is difficult, to be sure, but it is often the only path to peace. It may be important to restate here that there are situations where peace is *not* the goal, or at least is not the goal right now—situations in which the demands of justice or change take precedence over the restoration of a relationship; situations in which anger needs to be sustained, not set aside. But when peace between us is the goal, forgiveness is a powerful ally; sometimes it is our only hope.

There are times when it seems we cannot talk enough or explain enough or regret enough to bring us back together. The harm has been too heavy, the distance between us is now too great to be bridged. In such situations we relearn that the power of forgiveness is more than personal achievement; we are taught that it is often a gift and a grace that, spent by our anger, we must await in hope.

Reflective Exercises

Take some time now to recall your own experience of anger over the recent weeks and months. Let the memories return—the situations, the people, the circumstances that have been involved.

Then select two or three of these experiences that strike you as typical, as instances of the ways in which you are frequently aroused to anger. Spend some time with each of these, exploring your experience of anger in each. Can you recall the physical side of the anger, how your body felt in these situations? Was there a sense of injustice, an experience of humiliation, a threat to your self-esteem? Take time to trace the patterns of your own experience of anger.

What do you learn here about the virtue of anger? In what ways is this adult strength maturing in your own life? What strategies work best for you in the expression of anger? How do you move through anger toward forgiveness and reconciliation?

❧ 10 ❧

Passages in
Homosexual Holiness

A major metaphor of Christian life, vigorously reclaimed since
Vatican Council II, is that of journey. More than a figment of romantic imagination, this image captures our sense of being on the way
and of being accompanied and guided by someone.

Journey, as a metaphor of religious life, suggests the necessary
mobility and peril, the discoveries and losses that pattern our
Christian lives. As a people, our religious travels began with
Abraham leaving home. This image of journey has been even more
strongly imprinted on our souls since the Exodus—that generation
of desert travel during which our destination and traveling companions began to be revealed. The Israelite experience of journey—in
the Exodus, Exile, and Diaspora—was echoed in Jesus' itinerant
movement: "When Jesus had finished instructing his twelve disciples
he moved on from there to teach and preach in their towns"
(Matthew 11:1).

Christian history, like that of the Jews, is patterned by a deep
ambivalence. A desire to settle down, sink roots, establish a stable
life is experienced in tension with the need to move on, following a
revelation with endless surprises and turns. The metaphors of
Christian life display this ambivalence: "pilgrimage" is countered by
Augustine's image of a "City of God," a stable, well-boundaried
municipality. An awareness of the continuing journey of the "people
of God" exists alongside the sturdier conviction that "a mighty
fortress is our God." We yearn for a secure, well-defended place to

be with each other and with God. But each construction site ("Let us build three tents here" [Luke 9:33]) tends to become in time an archeological site—a place where God once had been. We Christians are settlers and builders, but our fidelity is pledged, since Abraham and Moses, to a mobile God whose revelations require uprooting and repeated departures.

As Christians we recognize our lives as journeys; we also believe them to be excursions with a direction and purpose. But what is this direction? Where are we going? The metaphor of journey contains another image that reveals something about the direction and the dynamic of our movement as a people. This is the image of passage. Since this notion was reintroduced by the Dutch anthropologist Arnold Van Gennep at the beginning of this century, Christian scholars have been exploring the passages that pattern modern religious maturing. Apart from the classic passages of birth, adult initiation, marriage, and death, other perilous transitions appear in our lives. Each of these passages, as a critical period of opportunity and danger, shapes the direction of our life journey.

The Dynamic of a Passage

In this chapter we examine three passages that homosexual Christians often face in the movement into maturity. Before doing that, it may be helpful to examine the peculiar dynamic of a passage by recalling two transitions common in adult life: the death of a parent and the establishment of a deep friendship. The central paradox of a passage is always loss and gain: it is a time of peril and possibility. During a passage we become vulnerable to both personal loss and unexpected grace. In the death of a parent we lose our beginnings and our security. That buffer between us and the world, that guarantor of meaning and security (which we may have experienced as often in conflict as in affection) is taken from us. We are, at last, orphaned. Stripped gradually or suddenly of this important person—this part of myself—I may well become disoriented, alone on my life journey in a new and frightening way.

In the very different experience of a beginning friendship, a similar dynamic is at play: amid the excitement and enthusiasm of a deepening relationship, we may feel a growing threat. If I admit this person into my heart, I will have to change. This is not because I am selfish or shallow but simply because my heart will have a new occupant. Most threatened, perhaps, is my sense of independence: to allow you into my life, I will have to let go of some of how I have been until now. Some part of who—and how—I have been will have to be let go if this new friendship and love is to grow. Naturally, then, I may hesitate. I may step back and choose not to undergo the threat of this passage of intimacy. In the face of the threat of a passage, then, we may resist. Our parent's death we cannot prevent, though we can deny its happening and refuse the passage that it instigates. And we can refuse the passage of friendship, feeling the risk to be too severe.

A passage begins, then, in disorientation and the threat of loss. It matures into a second stage as we allow ourselves to fully experience and name this loss. This middle part of a passage may endure for several months or even a year or more. In the reluctant, gradual letting go of a parent, or in the slow, gingerly admittance of a friend, we are losing ourselves and finding ourselves. But the terror of a passage appears in this in-between time: How do I know I can survive without the security and dependability of my parent (even an antagonistic parent)? How can I be sure that this growing friendship will be better than my well-defended independence? In the disorientation and darkness of a passage, I cannot see the other side. I cannot be sure, cannot control, where this journey leads.

The imagery of passage being used here is that favored by anthropologist Victor Turner and others: passage as a narrow, dark, subterranean journey. It is something that we "undergo"; Turner speaks of it as "cunicular," or tunnel-like. In exercises of guided fantasy, people often picture their life transitions in a very different fashion: a passage as an oceangoing voyage, as a leaving home and a setting out into uncharted waters. While this imagery of voyage includes the peril and unknown of the tunnel, it is strikingly different in its sense of openness, fresh air, and adventure. The nature of a specific crisis may dispose us toward certain imagery. The death of a child is likely to be experienced as a dark passage, a "valley of death" that must be gone through. A career change may be experienced as a frightening but exciting launching out into unknown waters. Both "passages" include leaving the familiar, traveling for a time while uncertain about the destination, and—for the Christian— expecting to meet God along the way.

The peculiar dynamic of a passage becomes clear in this movement of loss and discovery. Psychologically, we grow by letting go parts of ourselves no longer necessary for our journey; we are purified of parts of ourselves that do not fit the future. The reliance on parents once so necessary, and the personal independence we develop in young adulthood, must both eventually be let go if we are to grow into the authority of our own adult lives and into mature intimacy. But the reordering of our life that a passage promotes is also a disordering. The British anthropologist Mary Douglas writes about the "potency of disorder." And this potency is not only psychological but religious. This time of vulnerability and loss is also a time of potential grace. In the threat and even chaos of a life passage, we experience the opportunity for extraordinary growth. We find unsuspected strengths; we are startled by our ability to risk and to trust. And often it is only with hindsight that we identify the gracefulness of a time of passage. From that threat and loss we emerge not just different—and wounded—but stronger. In the darkness of that passage (or in the uncharted waters of our voyage) we find a new direction to or confidence in our life.

This experience of the grace of a passage illumines its third stage: emergence and reincorporation into the community. In the course of a passage we are likely to feel ourselves removed from the community. The disorientation makes us feel different; we withdraw and want to be left alone. Only gradually do we come to a renewed sense of ourselves—as able to go on without a loved one or to sustain the strains and excitement of intimacy. This renewal and reordering invites us out of the passage, bringing us back to the community, changed and matured. Traditionally, rites of passage have celebrated this newness—the adolescent is now an adult; these two individuals are a new community in marriage.

Some human passages we anticipate and celebrate easily in rites and rituals. Other passages are less expected and may remain hidden and disguised. When unexpected and hidden, a transition may be deprived of the rites of passage which identify and celebrate this movement. The three passages of homosexual maturing are of this type.

As we explore these passages, we will examine how the church might more gracefully structure rites of passage to facilitate these challenging life transitions. Whatever the passage, both human wisdom and Christian conviction tell us these transitions are not to be navigated alone. A central function of a believing community is to protect and guide its members through these harrowing and graceful periods.

Three Passages of Maturing

A major challenge in any crisis is to be able to imagine it. We search for metaphors and images which can give shape and direction to the confusing movements of our heart. We have already available to us an image of perilous transition for maturing homosexuals: coming out of the closet. This movement shares many characteristics of a traditional passage. Before examining how coming out may entail three different movements, we might recall the origin of this transition.

The closet is the starting point for the passage of coming out. This space shares many features of a womb: protective and dark, it is an excellent hiding place. It is at once secure and confining. Both womb and closet are important developmental havens meant to be outgrown. But to venture out of such secure confinement is to initiate a dangerous and exciting lifelong journey.

The psychological and religious development of the gay or lesbian adult may invite three different passages from three distinct closets. In examining the features of these transitions, we may find clues to the rites of passage through which the Christian community will minister more effectively to maturing homosexuals.

An Interior Passage

This first passage is more like a revolution and conversion. A lesbian Christian, gradually or suddenly, comes to understand and embrace herself for who she is. This is a passage from the closet of ignorance or denial to the light of self-acceptance. After perhaps years of avoiding the inner movements of affection and attraction, I feel myself invited to let go of the charade I have been playing with myself and to accept and befriend my own sexual identity. This is a passage of identity and vocation—coming to admit and love who I am and who I am called to be.

This passage will, expectably, be terrifying for many adults. Our culture and our church have reinforced the self-denial that keeps gay persons in the dark, even to themselves. To listen to and to own the movements of affection in my heart places me in great jeopardy. Here we see again the peculiar paradox of a passage: I am invited to let go of some cherished or accustomed part of myself, but will I survive the loss? If I admit to myself the direction of my desires, do I enter a passage or a dead end? In the midst of this passage—the only route to the maturing of my adult identity and vocation—I know the doubts experienced by our religious ancestors in the Sinai Desert. Nostalgia for the security of my former life (even if it was slavery) struggles against an insistence toward the insecure freedom of a new life.

This interior passage is a movement to self-intimacy. I am invited to acknowledge and embrace the person I am, with the enduring affections, desires, and feelings which constitute my self. This passage is interior in two senses: it takes place *within* the individual (though often spurred or threatened by social events), and it can take place apart from questions of interpersonal expressions of affection and commitment. Whatever decisions I will come to concerning the expression of my affection, I am invited in this first passage to befriend myself as *this* homosexual person created and loved by God.

This first passage differs from the later transitions in its foundational and nonnegotiable aspects. All of our adult love and work hinge on the self-knowledge and self-intimacy released in this passage. Those Christians who over many years find themselves to be predominantly and enduringly homosexual must come to accept and love this important part of themselves. To refuse this passage, to turn back because of the terror of this transition, is to choose a self-denial of a most unchristian form. To deny the existence and goodness of my affections and of my affective orientation must necessarily twist my adult efforts of love and work and thus must diminish my vocation.

This statement may seem too strong. Do we humans not survive with all kinds of strange strategies and compromises? The force of our insistence here is on the *interior* aspect of this passage: religious maturity means nothing if it does not include self-awareness and self-intimacy, a loving if mellow embrace of this person I am finding myself to be. In the closet of self-rejection we can be obedient children, fulfilling every church law, but we cannot become adult believers.

If this passage is so crucial, what about its timing and its possible failures? Both psychological research and pastoral experience suggest that this passage of identity is, for many Christians, a delayed passage. Psychologist Douglas Kimmel suggests that a homosexual person's self-identification often occurs in the early twenties; pastoral experience might adjust this timing for many Catholics into their middle or late twenties.

This delay in coming to a (somewhat) clear self-recognition as homosexual has both positive and problematic features. Problems can arise for young lesbian and gay Christians making life choices before they have negotiated this passage of sexual identity. The timing of this passage—and for some it is delayed until their thirties or even later—does not necessarily precipitate disaster, but it does mean that some important life experiences and commitments will demand later reappraisal and reintegration in light of this delayed passage.

But this delay may also have positive aspects. A danger for the adolescent or young adult, noted by many psychologists and counselors, is that of identity foreclosure: several homosexual experiences in the middle or late teens may convince a young person that he or she is constitutionally homosexual. He or she may then move into an explicitly gay lifestyle, prematurely closing off or "foreclosing" an identity that is still unclear and developing. The accumulated experience required to recognize and to begin to accept my sexual identity as predominantly and enduringly homosexual usually requires some years of adult living. Daniel Levinson's research into patterns of early adult development, circumscribed though his study is, suggests convincingly that many people today require most of the decade of their twenties to come to a sense of adult identity. Increasingly, religious counselors are inviting young Catholics to take the time required to come to a firm sense of their sexual identity. The timing of this movement of identity is crucial but varies greatly. Some must confront this initial passage in their late teens, others not until a decade or more later. And this timing can be frustrated by both foreclosure (judging prematurely that I am gay or straight) and denial (refusing to accept the accumulating experience which reveals me to myself).

The notion of timing brings us to the question of rites of passage, reminding us that such an event is a potentially sacred time. This time of self-examination and loss is also a period of opportunity and grace. Here, in the recognition of this passage as graceful, the church's ministry to homosexual maturing begins. So frightened have we been of the homosexual members of our mystical body that we have ignored the graces that accompany so many homosexual Christians' quiet interior passage to self-acceptance. In the place of rites of passage we have isolated our ministry in the private, often hidden caring that was given in such closet-like settings as the confessional. A complication here is that "rites of passage" are generally public events in which we acknowledge, invoke, and celebrate the action of God's grace, while this first passage, as we have been considering it, is essentially interior and individual. How shall we protect its privacy without rendering it secretive? We do make this passage public when we sponsor community discussions of homosexual maturing; we give this crisis visibility when we recognize it as one of the patterned modes of grace and maturity within the Christian community. A growing body of theological and pastoral writing itself is a kind of rite in which this first interior passage and other graceful events in the lives of our lesbian and gay members are brought to light and celebrated. These public discussions of the patterns of homosexual religious maturing are rites that "routinize" gay Christian life—making it less exceptional or even less "bizarre," and more a variant route among the many journeys we undertake with and toward God.

Finally, the recognition of this passage as a crucial period of grace in young adult life has a developmental value. When we negotiate a crisis successfully we not only survive, we grow stronger. We are strengthened for the journey and its subsequent challenges. Psychologically speaking, growth in a sense of identity strengthens us to love well and work effectively. Religiously speaking, our graceful embrace of our identity becomes the strength of our vocation as we come to know and love who we are and who we are being called to be. This confidence in our religious identity, our vocation, supports all our subsequent efforts of Christian intimacy and our life work.

A Passage of Intimacy

A second passage appears in the life journey of homosexuals when they experience an invitation or challenge to share themselves with others. In the interior passage I am being invited to a deeper acceptance and love of *myself;* in this second passage I am being led to a mode of presence with *others* where I am known for who I am. These passages may occur at the same time, yet we can distinguish these two different challenges: in the one, self-acceptance, and in the other, the need and desire to be known and loved for who I am. The danger and ambiguity of this second passage appears in the conflict between a growing desire to share myself and the apprehension that such sharing might mean rejection and humiliation. As the desire to share myself grows, the question arises—With whom will I do this sharing? Dare I tell my friend of many years this secret, vulnerable part of who I am? A woman religious wonders whether to share this part of her heart with her spiritual director. A gay priest wants to but hesitates to share his sexual identity with other priests in his support group. A young adult would like to share this part of herself with her family.

In the traversing of this passage I gradually let go the safety of not being known, the security of sexual anonymity. Strengthened by a growing comfort with myself (the grace of the first passage), I am encouraged to depart from this protective anonymity and enter the risk, and excitement, of being known as I am. I am invited out of a second closet.

The timing of this passage merits special scrutiny. For many gay and lesbian Christians the first tentative steps of social intimacy (as distinguished from self-intimacy) happen in the middle or late twenties. The delay of this passage of intimacy, like that of the first passage, has both problematic and positive features. One problematic aspect is the accumulated experience of *not* being known by my closest friends and colleagues. This history of sexual anonymity, as it grows, may make it more difficult to "come out" in any interpersonal way. A positive aspect of this delay is that it may allow for a steadily increasing comfort with and love of myself. This returns us to the interrelationship of these two passages. Whatever our sexual inclinations, we learn about our loveliness by being loved. It is most often others who first announce to us the surprising news of our goodness and attractiveness. Yet our adult ability to love well—that is, to share our lives and bodies in honest and nonmanipulative ways—rests on an enduring confidence in our own loveliness. Convincing myself that God loves me when I do not love myself is a most difficult task. The lessons of my loveliness, learned from others and from God, must take root in me as a dependable conviction: this is the meaning of virtue.

Common in both gay and straight experience is the plunge into the passage of interpersonal intimacy without first traversing the interior passage of self-acceptance. We announce ourselves, uncover ourselves to others, in the hope that if they love us we may be brought to accept ourselves. Often such efforts arise from a too powerful dependence on others and a deep distrust of ourselves. The busy, if not frenzied, activity of the narcissistic person parodies this second passage: revealing myself to others again and again, I hope to learn who I am. Having sidestepped the earlier passage and lacking confidence in and comfort with oneself, the narcissistic person deals in facile self-revelation and instant intimacy. But this activity of self-disclosure and sharing, which at first appears to be the work of this second passage, never takes hold. The grace of this passage—a sustained and enduring relationship—never occurs, because such persons do not love themselves.

We have described this passage as one of intimacy. By this we mean the psychological and religious resources which allow us to sustain the ambiguities, excitement, and strain of being up close to others. A passage of intimacy is a period for both testing and developing these strengths. This passage is necessary for so many homosexuals today precisely because it is so difficult to continually come up close in friendship and in work while keeping closeted this important part of oneself. These strengths of intimacy, tested and released in this passage, rescue us from a too-intense privacy. Decisions about sexual and genital expressions of intimacy are separable from this movement of intimacy; whether Christian adults choose a celibate or a sexually active lifestyle, they must face this passage. In this deepest sense of the word, intimacy is not optional.

If the timing of this passage and its relationship to the prior passage are important, so is the context in which it occurs. Context returns us to the question of rites of passage. What environments support or endanger this passage? Can we imagine rites by which our church might more gracefully minister to this expectable passage in the life journey of its members?

This passage happens for some Catholics in the context of spiritual direction. As this context itself continues to be transformed (from a sin-oriented exchange between priest and "penitent" to a development-oriented exchange between the adult Christian and a religious guide), this sharing of one's homosexual identity occurs in a more supportive environment. The growth of Dignity, Integrity, and similar organizations within Christian denominations over the past decade has offered an explicitly religious context for gay and lesbian Christians to meet others. The increase of retreats available for homosexual Christians adds another social context for this passage of psychological and religious intimacy. Because this second passage remains a somewhat private movement—the sharing of one's sexual identity with close friends or special intimates—the rites of passage will expectably take place in supportive contexts rather than in the more public settings implied in the more traditional use of this term.

We can come to a greater clarity about the subtle but crucial effects of rites of passage by reflecting on their dual purpose: to protect and to predict. Rites represent the community's concern to protect individuals at critical periods of life. Thus the Rite of Baptism protects the new Christian at the critical point of dying to a former way of life and being born to a Christian style of life. The rites of puberty in many social groups are intended to protect the young person in the dangerous transition toward adult responsibility. Through organizations such as New Ways Ministry, through retreats and other support groups, the believing community protects gay and lesbian Catholics who are struggling to let themselves be known and to develop a style of intimacy at once homosexual and Christian. These rites protect individuals from the culture's scorn, from isolation, and from having to experience this transition alone and in private.

As rites of passage protect, they also predict. They help the individual to focus on the challenge being faced, and they announce that the person will survive. Here the accumulated wisdom of the community ministers to an individual's experience: "This passage, which you experience as unique and special, has happened before. God is at work here." The community's care and attention tell us we will come through. The community witnesses to what God is about in such passages. God strips us of a once necessary anonymity and calls us to share ourselves with others. In its rites a community encourages us to let go and to trust this process of purification and growth. This contribution of the community is crucial because our individual experiences are so limited. If I let go part of myself—such as the security of being unknown—how can I trust that this will lead to a better, more mature way of living? This is a question that the community is able to, or should be able to, answer. Over the past three thousand years and more, we have learned the patterns of

God's action: life from death, gain from loss, grace from crisis. An ungraceful part of our recent religious history has been the community's denial of homosexual maturing. With such a denial, the believing community forfeits its role of protecting and predicting this pattern of religious growth. Thus homosexual Christian maturity has remained closeted, hidden. Thus "darkened," it could not perform its generative function: to witness to the next generation the shape, the perils, and the graces of this Christian journey. This brings us to the third passage.

A Public Passage

For some gay and lesbian Christians, a third passage appears in their life journey. This is the transition into being recognized as homosexual and Christian in the public world. This public passage is religious when it includes coming out as homosexual *and Christian.* While the interior passage cannot be ignored, this public passage need not be undertaken by all homosexual Christians. There are perils that attend the public acknowledgment of oneself as gay. Recriminations from society and from the church still make it inadvisable for many homosexuals to be publicly known as such. Most homosexual Christians who have matured through the first passage of self-acceptance and have risked the second passage of intimacy with a few others continue to grow in the ways of Christ without coming out publicly. But for some, this third passage demands attention.

What are the possible motives inclining one to make this passage? One obvious motive is a compulsive desire to be seen and recognized. While such exhibitionism is not a motive reserved for gay life, what often lingers in the public mind is the outrageous costumes and intentionally shocking display of some gay rights demonstrations. And although judgments about the political usefulness of these demonstrations differ, one disservice of such display is to distract public view from others who bear more realistic and less ostentatious witness to the gay lifestyle.

A very different motive may impel other gays and lesbians whose public actions, whether in settings of work or politics or community discussion, disclose their sexual identity. At the other pole of the motivational continuum from exhibitionism is the motive of generativity. By this word, borrowed from Erik Erikson, we mean the impulse, felt with special urgency in midlife, to care for and to contribute to the next generation. The most common example of this dynamic and its strength is, of course, parenting. From our twenties through our fifties we are especially concerned, as parents, with providing a livable future for our children. As this strength matures into a virtue, we come to care not only for our own, but for the children of the world.

But this human instinct and Christian virtue is not biologically bound. The maturing of the celibate and unmarried Christian invites attention to this same impulse. And so this virtuous instinct will lead some lesbian and gay Christians to come out publicly. In so doing, their life and vocation become a public witness of homosexual and Christian maturing and a gift to the next generation. Such a life provides, for both homosexual and heterosexual Christians, an image of what it is to mature as Christian and gay. Such a witness is generative because it provides a publicly observable model of homosexual Christian life. This is not a model in a legal or normative sense—"this is how lesbian or gay Christians *must* act"—it is a model in a more heuristic sense. Where there was once a void ("Do *you* know any gay Christians?"), patterns of Christian homosexual maturing begin to appear. It is possible! It becomes publicly imaginable to be both homosexual and a mature Christian. Many believers have known this for some time, but it was information not publicly available; it was not part of the church's social imagination. Closeted lives, however holy, cannot provide images and models of religious maturing. A certain public exposure and light is required for this virtue of generativity to have its effect.

Some Catholics will feel called to make this third passage of maturity. The very real dangers of this transition require an extraordinary personal resilience developed in the previous passages. Again, timing is crucial, as a negative example may best illustrate. A young homosexual man may, after some years of denying his sexual identity, suddenly burst out of this repression. Attempting all three passages simultaneously, he joins several gay groups, declaring his identity to anyone who will listen. In a single, emphatic coming out he pursues the tasks of three passages: public witness, interpersonal intimacy, self-acceptance. In his public self-disclosure, he is hoping to be accepted—by society, by his family and friends, and by himself. The special challenge of this third passage argues that we enter it only when strengthened by the awareness and support gained over the years that are usually involved in making the earlier passages.

How can a person decide about this third passage? How do I know if I am being called to this more public transition? In the first, interior passage it is the strength and virtue of my vocation that is released: I come to accept and love this particular person who I am and the life journey which is my own. During the months or years of this passage, I come to a greater confidence in what God is about in my life. During the second passage another virtue is tested—Christian intimacy. I learn gradually to risk myself in coming close to others, and I begin to construct the style of intimacy and interpersonal commitment that fits my vocation. These virtues of vocation and intimacy will be crucial to see the Christian through the public passage of coming out. One cannot enter this passage simply because it is "the thing to do" or because others have made it. A Christian enters it because he is invited to do so, because he senses himself so called. Many Christians are not asked to make this public passage. Others, because of the particular circumstances and special graces of their lives, will be invited, lured, goaded into this passage. What rites of passage can the believing community provide to assist this transition?

The rites for this public passage will also be of a contextual nature rather than more specific public rituals. Few of us at this point in the life of the church can imagine a ritual celebration at a parish coming-out party. A rite that is beginning to appear, however, is the establishment of parish and diocesan committees for ministry to and with homosexual Catholics. Such a structural event is a rite in that it publicly announces (and so, to some extent, authorizes) the existence of these members of the believing community. An example of such a rite has been the recent establishment, in several dioceses across the country, of a special task force concerned with ministry to lesbian and gay Catholics. The existence and activity of such official groups made public the gay and lesbian members of the Catholic community. In so doing, they begin the process of protecting and predicting this public passage. Practically, it becomes more possible now for gay and lesbian Catholics to serve publicly on this task force. In acknowledging the existence of and then creating public space for homosexual Catholics to stand in the community, the church facilitates this third, public passage. In doing this the church senses, though not without some anxiety and self-doubt, that it is these maturing lesbian and gay Christians who will witness to believers the shape of homosexual holiness.

Passages and Exits

The journey of Christian maturing is patterned with many different passages. We are a people in movement, pledged to and in pursuit of a not always discernible God. Movement and change, then, are the essence of religious growth. Grace (hints of God's presence and pleasure) breaks into our lives in periods of crisis and loss. In the passages into marriage, at the death of a loved one, approaching retirement, or in coming out, we are stripped of some previously important part of ourselves. Forced to let go of what once seemed so essential, we discover new parts of ourselves. We stumble onto strengths and resources we had not suspected. We are invited to leave home again and again; we find ourselves with fewer possessions and more flexibility as we travel with our sometimes elusive God. And in the repeated purifications of our life, we begin to learn that this is how we grow into the maturity of Jesus Christ. We thought (we had been taught!) that the journey would be more "normal," more orthodox. But it hardly ever is. As we gradually recognize the astounding variegation in our journeys with God, we also come to identify the common elements in our different passages.

Becoming more adept at our shared journey, we are beginning to see that some human movements we had named "exits" are more often passages of grace. Two such exits are the movements of divorce and of coming out. In a church suspicious that adult change is likely to be tainted by error or sin, these movements were interpreted as exits. Divorce appeared to be, in essence, a chosen religious infidelity; as such, it could not be a passage of grace. Homosexuality was seen as a chosen unnatural disposition; as such, to be homosexual meant to be unholy. Like divorce, it was a necessary departure or exit from faith and grace.

Gradually we believers have been confronted with the evidence: mature members of our communities of faith divorce (most often with much pain and regret and guilt), but they do not by that event leave their faith or their maturity. Sometimes they seem to grow more mature and holy. They seem (dare we say it?) to be graced by their divorce. Likewise gay and lesbian Christians: coming to cherish themselves and strengthened to pursue responsible lives of love and commitment, many become more mature believers as well. Embracing their sexual identity leads them not out of the church but more deeply into it. We are finally seeing, then, that these life experiences need not be exits but may often be passages of grace. If these have become passages of grace for many despite the deafening silence of the church's official ministry, how graceful might they become in a church bold enough to confess the movement of God in these passages?

Finally, it might be instructive to observe some parallels between these three passages and the maturing of the church itself in its ministry to its homosexual members. The church's gradual movement from a denial of Christian homosexual maturing to a private acceptance (in the confessional and individual counseling) of the gay and lesbian Christian represents a kind of interior passage. In an exercise of self-intimacy, the church acknowledged—at least individually and privately—the holiness of some of its lesbian and gay members. A typical approach during this period of the church's maturing ministry was to affirm God's love for the homosexual while counseling a celibate lifestyle.

As the church itself matured, growing more aware of and comfortable with different parts of its own body, its ministry began to endorse more enthusiastically the goodness of human intimacy, even for homosexual Christians. It began to bless, though in a very private and hidden way, the life of the homosexual couple. Here the theological logic was that such a life was a lesser evil than its alternatives. The public statements of the church at this stage conflicted with its maturing "private practice." The parallels are not strong, but we may see this stage of the church's ministry as representing a second passage. Responsible intimacy was recognized as an important part of maturing for the homosexual Christian, but this recognition was not public.

The establishment of diocesan task groups, the recognition of organizations such as Dignity and New Ways Ministry, the planning of pastoral conferences on the topic, the scheduling of retreats for lesbian and gay Christians—these efforts have begun to move the church toward a new stage of ministerial maturity. Tentatively the church is now approaching this third passage. Its public statements are more sophisticated and graceful; generalizations and homophobic overtones are diminishing. We are beginning to acknowledge that our own body, the Body of Christ, is in part gay. Nor are these homosexual parts of the Christian body now seen only as immature or a cause of shame. As the church itself matures, as it becomes more in touch with its own body, with all this body's wounds and strengths, it makes possible the public witness of those lifestyles that can reveal to all of us the shape of homosexual holiness and maturity.

Reflective Exercises

Care begins in awareness. Spend some time now with your awareness of gay and lesbian Christians. What is your initial reaction to the word *homosexual*—fear, confusion, recognition? How aware are you of the lesbian and gay Christians among your circle of friends, your work associates, in the parish and elsewhere?

How does the Christian community closest to you respond to its gay and lesbian members? Are they welcome? Is the atmosphere one of silence, of rejection, of support?

How might this community of faith nurture the spiritual growth of lesbian and gay Christians? For example, making available structured opportunities in the community for homosexual members to find support and, if necessary, healing? Encouraging discussion groups or retreats or days of prayer? How can the community itself be helped to celebrate the presence among us of Christians who are gay?

❧ PART THREE ❧

Power and Intimacy: Paths of Maturity

Wherever we travel in adult life, we find ourselves on the paths of power and intimacy. Growing more powerful, we are still stumped by our enduring weakness. And we are compelled to negotiate differences in power—unequal strengths in a marriage, the shifting balance of power in a parish. In our common life, authority appears as the social face of power: in our judgments about legitimate authority, we affirm the shape of God's power among us and decide who is in charge. Power and authority are the focus of Chapter Eleven and Chapter Twelve.

The second path of maturing is intimacy—that ability to sustain the ambiguities of being up close to others in love and work. A special challenge in the church today is the cooperation of women and men in ministry. In Chapter Thirteen we examine some of the dynamics of conflict and tension in this aspect of Christian intimacy. In the final chapter we touch the most mellow mode of intimacy—absence. This often disguised face of intimacy awaits us in the loss of loved ones and in the unexplained absence of God at different periods of our lives.

11

Reimagining Personal Power

"Stir up your power, O Lord, and come." In this Advent prayer we invoke God's power and invite it into our lives. As we mature, our own power is stirred; both virtue and confidence grow strong. But if it is obvious that Christian maturing is about power, it is also unnerving. We have been schooled in a reluctance about power. We experience power interiorly in surges of anger and sexual arousal. Although these forces are healthy, they are also frequently frightening. Our social imaginations are wounded by the devastating shape that power has taken in public: the overshadowing cloud of Hiroshima; the scent of Auschwitz; the sights of Vietnam. Power seems demonic, so often destructive.

Lord Acton's judgment comes quickly to mind: "Power tends to corrupt, and absolute power corrupts absolutely." If this is so, then becoming holy must mean avoiding power and its corruptions. But even as we cling to safer ideals of meekness and humility of heart, we sense we have succumbed to a narrow view of power. Can power be rescued from this solely negative interpretation? Power is destructive—and creative. Power is demonic—and holy. Can this rich ambiguity be recovered and celebrated as a part of Christian life? In the following pages we will explore the experience of power in adult life for clues to its shape as a Christian virtue.

We saw in Chapter Six that the word *virtue* means, simply, "power." We recalled that Yahweh answered to the name of Power in the Hebrew Scriptures. A more imaginative look at the New Testament suggests that it is a story about power: God's power, become tangible in Jesus Christ, seeks to season our lives in various gifts and virtues. And Lord Acton's statement finds its complement in the Gospel accounts of Jesus: power tends to heal, and absolute power heals absolutely. Jesus' words give hope, and his touch heals. By his life he announces a power that knows no limit to its healing. If we can imagine power as more than corrupting, we can begin to explore its role in Christian maturing. In this exploration we may come to recognize the shape of personal power in our own lives, as our real but limited strengths grow into reliable virtues.

Power is about strength. And strength comes in various shapes in the different contexts of our lives. Among teenagers, for example, the most important sign of strength may be athletic ability or good looks. In a suburban neighborhood, it may be the prestige of my occupation or the size of my paycheck. And the world community watches with concern as nations vie for superiority in the destructive strengths of war.

Discussions of power are complicated and often confusing. Two clarifications can assist our efforts to understand the place of power in our lives. First, it is misleading to treat power as a thing, as though it were an internal "packet" of energy. Power is not an entity but a way of interacting. Power is more a process than a thing. Power points to something that happens *between* people, something going on, an interaction. Power is not so much a possession as a way of relating.

Second, it is useful to distinguish between *personal* power and *social* power. Personal power points to my awareness of *myself* as strong, the ways I find myself capable or coercive in interaction with others. Social power refers to the broader experiences of strength *among* us—the energy in this group, the authority of this organization. Social power also involves an awareness of the differences in strength among us—what these differences are and how we will deal with them. We do not all possess equally the kinds of strength that are seen as important in *this* group, whether they be intelligence or goodness or money or political clout. The patterns of social power in any group reflect the ways that members recognize and negotiate these differences in strength.

Social power and personal power are closely related. It is in a group—in the family or on a work team or as a member of a civic organization—that most of us become aware of our own power. The definitions of power in these groups (social power) influence my awareness of how I am strong (personal power). The group's sense of the strengths that are worthwhile often becomes the criterion I use to judge whether I am powerful. The influence can also go in the other direction. When there are changes in an awareness of personal power, the patterns of social authority and group leadership shift as well. We have examples of this in the current experience of the church, as women religious seek new roles of leadership and responsibility in diocesan structures, and as laypersons look for new patterns of dialog and accountability in their relationship with the clergy. Acknowledging these connections between personal and social power, we focus our discussion here on personal power. We take up several questions of social power in the next chapter, in a discussion of authority and obedience.

The Faces of Personal Power

Power, we have suggested, is not a possession but a social transaction. It is one of the ways in which we come face-to-face as adults. Care, conflict, and control—each is an experience of power through which we touch each other and influence one another's lives. This interaction of personal power wears at least five faces.

FACES OF PERSONAL POWER

Mode	Experienced as	Needed in
Power On	initiative and influence	adult competence
Power Over	coordination and control	organizational leadership
Power Against	competition and conflict	assertion and negotiation
Power For	service and nurturance	parenthood and ministry
Power With	mutuality and collaboration	interdependence and dependability

Power On

We see the first face of power in our acts of initiation and influence: "Things happen because of me." It may be a very simple act: I find I can make another person smile. It may be a more complex exercise of influence: I present a new plan at work, and it receives serious consideration. Or in a troubled friendship, I risk a confrontation that moves our relationship to a deeper level.

"Power on" is the simplest, most innocent face of power. I find I can do things; my actions make a difference. I am more than a child or a passive victim. I can influence my world—at least in some ways. This first experience of power does not yet confront the difference between care and constraint or feel the tension between influence and coercion.

But even this simplest form of power is not always easy to attain. A variety of factors can defeat this personal strength. A dominating parent may so manage my life that I am left with no sense of autonomous power: I am cared for, but I cannot shape my own world. Or poverty may educate me in impotence: I am too weak, too ineffectual to influence others. I am encouraged to see myself as a victim, unable to be powerful except, perhaps, in self-destructive acts of violence.

Through the experience of "power on," I come to sense that I am an agent in my own life and that I have resources which enable me to influence my environment. My strength is not simply "housed" within me, it moves beyond me to influence people and events. I am strong enough to have an impact.

"Power on" gives me a basic sense of my own autonomy and adequacy. It leads to an appreciation of my special competence: I do some things well. This sense of effectiveness gives me confidence to take on the responsibilities of adult life, both in love and in work. Having a skill, mastering a difficult task, being able to bring a project to completion—each of these can bring with it a perception of myself as strong, as having resources that can be counted on to see me through.

Paradoxically, such mature autonomy is a foundation of adult intimacy as well. Marriage and family counselors know how much the conviction "I can make it on my own if I have to" is part of mature interdependent love. This strength of autonomy is not all that is involved; to grow in intimacy I must also be able to take the risk of not going it alone, of counting on you to be with me. But if I cannot trust my own resources, I am likely to become too dependent, insisting that you satisfy my needs because I do not feel adequate in myself.

Power Over

A second face of adult strength appears as we are challenged not just to influence others but to take charge. Many of the responsibilities of daily life require this kind of power. Serving on the parish council, disciplining our teenage children, supervising a production team, even returning a defective piece of merchandise—each of these is difficult for me if I have no sense of "power over," of the possibility and legitimacy of my giving direction to other people.

But "power over" often appears as a frowning face of power because it seems to suggest force and manipulation. Perhaps it is the word *over* that frightens us, conjuring up memories of bullies and bosses who used their power to dominate. For many of us, then, there are old wounds to be healed before we can move comfortably into the realm of leading others.

The earlier expression of power was in my own strength; I *can do* something. This second face of power introduces me to managing the power of others. To assume leadership in a group, I must be able to generate and focus energies that go beyond my own. (Caring for a family, too, requires the coordination and control of diverse and often conflicting energies. In any role of supervision—as foreman, as teacher, as mentor—I must be able to exercise "power over." Without this kind of power among us, much of group life seems ineffective. Decisions are not carried out, resources are wasted, energies dissipate.

Most of us recognize the importance of this face of personal power, but we remain uneasy with it. Our ambivalence about "power over" may lie in the very different images and feelings that surround its two functions of coordination and control.

The word *coordination* may call up images of a dance troupe. We are impressed and delighted by the coordination of each dancer's movements in the precision of the company's performance. In coordination we see the harmony of disparate powers unified in a graceful effort.

But *control* evokes more sinister images: arms that hold us too tightly, rules that restrict our freedom. It may help to recall that the seemingly effortless coordination of the athlete comes only with exceptional control. The dancer's grace comes only in a body that has been well controlled, exercised again and again in disciplined movement. This tedious repetition and control are concealed in the final artistic product but are the sure supports of the performance.

Control remains a suspect exercise of power, and with good reason. In our recent social memory, control has so often been exercised in constraint and coercion. Leadership positions have often been used to pursue private gain rather than the common good. In these instances, "power over" loses its necessary nuances of shared goals and mutual accountability. It comes to be a mask for manipulation.

If we know that control can lead to coercion, we must acknowledge that the two are not simply synonyms. Definitions of control include bringing together a number of resources; keeping a complicated effort on track; giving a sense of direction to a larger effort. These activities of control are essential in our life together. Without this kind of power among us it is difficult for us to celebrate our sense of cohesion as a family or to chart our future as a religious congregation.

To remind ourselves that the exercise of control is not always manipulative, we might recall the power of the conductor in an orchestra or of the director in a play. Each role requires "power over": the ability to focus a group's energies, to channel diverse resources into an organic whole. For the group to be successful, the leader must have control. But the leader's control exists in context. Both the conductor and the musicians are accountable to the musical score. The goal of the joint effort lies outside of the leader's control; it provides the criterion by which the leader's control can be judged. Both the group and the leader are accountable to something beyond their ultimate control. When "power over" is exercised in this way, in pursuit of a common goal and in the context of mutual accountability, it can resist the temptation toward manipulation.

Our ambivalence about control helps explain some of the tensions today over the function of leadership in the community of faith. Ministry often includes roles of organizational management and institutional leadership. Increasingly we see a reluctance among ministers to move into these roles. This kind of leadership can seem a thankless task. It demands skills of initiation and restraint, empowerment and accountability. Yet the very exercise of these resources of "power over" seems tainted. Both the leader and the group are keenly sensitive about attitudes and actions that give hints of control. Most leaders realize that their success depends to a large degree on the support of group members, both reinforcing their right to lead and cooperating in the decisions made. This support can be seriously compromised when every exercise of control is likely to be interpreted as coercion. In the face of such suspicion some leaders back away from the exercise of "power over." But without the freedom to exert "power over" when it is necessary, the burdens of organizational responsibility become overwhelming, even for talented and generous leaders. There are other talented people today who, knowing that a leadership position deprived of the resources of coordination and control is doomed to failure, refuse to take on this organizational role. In both instances, ministry suffers.

It is with good reason that we have been suspicious of organizational power. Yet there are signs in the church today that we are moving beyond this widespread suspicion of our leaders. In our dioceses and parishes and religious houses, we are slowly coming to realize that without coordination and control, our corporate effort is weakened. Little by little we are improving at distinguishing control from coercion: when leadership's control remains accountable to the common good, a good that is not interpreted solely by the leader, "power over" can be a graceful exercise of strength. Maturity requires not an abandonment of our suspicions of control but their clarification. We need to be able to welcome back among us the strength of "power over." This strength, like any other, requires accountability and ongoing purification. But without it we are weaker, both personally and communally.

Power Against

A third mode of power, equally troublesome for many of us, takes its stance "against." This is power in its combative face. I experience my strength when challenged by the people in my life or by the circumstances and obstacles I encounter. The awareness here includes an experience of struggle and opposition, even antagonism. At issue is whether I will be found adequate to the test, whether—in the face of some outside forces—my own strength will prevail.

This experience of power is a part of competitive games, where I match my strength and skill against that of an opponent. Winning, having my power prevail "against" my opponent, is important to me here. But as I learn to play well, I come to recognize that winning is not the only benefit involved in the game. There is the exhilaration of the contest itself, the opportunity to try my strength and further develop my skill. There is even the mellow lesson that I can lose without being humiliated and that I can fall without being shamed. Often the camaraderie of playing against one another is the chief benefit of the game, offering its own kind of companionship and intimacy.

To be sure, the game can degenerate into a struggle to win at whatever price, but it need not do so. And when a game does become such a battle, we often sense that energies have gone awry and that something important in the contest itself has been lost.

To be able to contest, then, is a part of adult maturity. It is a resource of adult power important not only in competitive sports but even more so in the movements of competition, confrontation, and conflict that are part of the exercise of adult responsibility.

Increasingly we are aware, from both the findings of psychological research and the evidence of our own lives, of the place of competition and conflict in "up close" relationships. Conflict between spouses, struggles between parents and their teenage children, antagonism among different groups in the parish—these are normal and expectable dynamics of living with others. These conflicts can escalate toward hostility and hatred: this is part of our fear of power used "against." But conflict is not *inevitably* destructive. This powerful part of life "up close" can be harnessed in a way that turns its energy to good use, redistributing power among us, revitalizing our commitment to one another, suggesting fresh alternatives for the future.

To deal maturely with these dynamics of competition and conflict I must be somewhat comfortable with the experience of myself as powerful "against." I must know that I am strong enough to stand in the face of another person's power and survive. I must be comfortable with my own power to such a degree that I can trust myself to handle my rage, to moderate my self-interest.

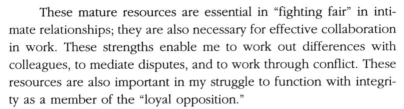

These mature resources are essential in "fighting fair" in intimate relationships; they are also necessary for effective collaboration in work. These strengths enable me to work out differences with colleagues, to mediate disputes, and to work through conflict. These resources are also important in my struggle to function with integrity as a member of the "loyal opposition."

With these resources of mature contesting, I know that I am strong enough to risk the fight, trusting that I will survive—whether I win or lose. This conviction gives me courage to enter the social arena with other powerful adults.

Power For

Another way in which I come to a sense of personal power is in an awareness that "I am strong for others." Many responsibilities of adulthood call out this special kind of strength. As a coworker, I give my talent to the tasks of the team. As a parent, I marshal my resources to care for my children. As a designated leader, I use my influence to further the goals of the group. My ability to have an impact and to make a difference is focused outside myself. I spend myself and my resources in pursuit of someone else's benefit.

At its best, this impulse is expressed in nurturance. I am powerful enough to participate in creating something new—our child or a joint project or a shared dream. Beyond this movement of creativity, I can use my power in care, in support of this new life on its own terms. The crucial phrase here, of course, is "on its own terms." The challenge of nurturance is to be able to use my power for others in ways that empower rather than diminish them, in ways that increase their freedom rather than make them more dependent on me.

We sense how tricky this can be for the parent, to care for growing children not by forcing them to become "my best idea" of who they should be but by fostering their growth into the persons they are in their own right. The task is no less tricky for the leader or the counselor or the person in ministry. Our responsibilities require us to use our power for other adults. We come in touch with the ambiguity involved in the use of our power "for their sake." This is the tension between care and constraint.

When I know myself to be strong in regard to another's need, a feeling of dominance may be provoked. Power and need are not shared between us. One of us may emerge as "strong" in the relationship and the other as "weak." This perception of a power imbalance can be destructive in a relationship between adults.

Mature relationships between adults are characterized by mutuality, even where strict "equality" is neither necessary nor possible. We cannot be exactly equal in intelligence, physical strength, social graces, and other abilities. The challenge of mutuality invites us to become engaged with each other's strengths and weaknesses. You can see and embrace both my strengths and my limits; I can acknowledge and support both your gifts and your weaknesses. Such mutuality neither demands nor pretends to be a total equality. By recognizing and even celebrating differences of strength, we protect ourselves from the genuine imbalances of paternalism and dependency. Without an active commitment to mutuality, I can gradually slip into identifying your good with my sense of "what is good for you." An attitude that begins in altruistic care can shift toward condescension. The illusion here is to judge that I know better than you what is in your best interests; it is a temptation to which many in ministry and other helping professions may be especially prone.

But "power for" remains an important resource of adult maturity. When the arrogance of "I know better than you what is in your best interests" can be recognized, the strengths of generative care can be released. These are essential for the responsibilities of parenting; they are crucial in religious leadership as well.

Power With

The fifth face of adult power is "power with." This experience is rooted in the conviction that "we are strong together." In our coming together, I know myself to be strong. Your strength does not diminish me or replace my own. Instead it increases and enhances my strength. My power is in part a strength that is shared. The experience here is that of interdependence—the ability to enjoy *mutual* influence and *mutual* empowerment. This resource draws on the matured strengths of dependability—a "depend-ability" that goes both ways.

For the benefits of interdependence to be available to me I must, first, *be able to depend on others*. I need the conviction, born in part of experience and in part of trust, that I do not have to do it by myself. This capacity for dependence is not the kind of *dependency* so feared by most Americans: the inability to care for my own needs that leaves me at the mercy of others. It is not the dependency that therapists see in the person who characteristically uses his needs to manipulate those around him. Rather it is a strength of dependence: I am strong enough to receive and benefit from others' power. It is because I know myself to be (somewhat) strong that I can allow my weaknesses to be visible to myself and to others as well. My weaknesses are not stronger than my strengths. So I need not consume my energies in the endless and futile effort to hide my limitations; I need not spend my strength in self-defense.

Such mature dependence is grounded in *having received* strength and nurturance from the outside, from other people in my environment. Having received this strength from beyond myself, I become strong enough now to meet my own needs and those of other people as well.

In work this enables me to trust your talent to supplement my own. I know that your abilities can compensate in areas where I am not strong. I can admit my limits and rejoice in the resources that you bring to our common tasks.

In the close relationships of friendship and marriage, I come to trust that your strength will be there for me when I need it. I learn that it is safe to share my vulnerability and to acknowledge how much I need you. I need not fear that this will lessen me in your eyes or that you will turn away in disgust. The adult strength of mutuality grows out of this shared ability to depend.

Interdependence requires that I be able to depend on others; it also demands that I be able *to let others depend on me.* This means that I can make my strength available in ways that empower others rather than diminish them. I am not intimidated by other people's strength, nor am I frightened by their weakness. I can be counted on by other people. I know how to let them lean on me without seducing them to become lasting dependents. I can care beyond control.

This sense of "power with," then, may be experienced in both love and collaboration. We count on each other to bring different resources to our common task. We rely on one another's strengths to make up for the limits we each have. And beyond this, we are aware that when we come together there is power available that goes beyond what was originally ours. In *Insight and Responsibility,*

Erik Erikson speaks of this experience of "power with." "In relationships of full mutuality, the sharing goes beyond self-disclosure toward interpenetration of lives . . . [as] partners depend on each other for the development of their respective strengths." In this family or diocese or congregation, our communal effort is richer because our powers have come together. The fruit of "power with" goes beyond the achievement of goals to include the enrichment of each of us and of our shared life.

Power and Weakness

Any serious discussion of maturity must confront both power and weakness. Adult life does not simply lead us out of impotence into strength. That is a fantasy of adolescence. Maturity asks, instead, a befriending of ourselves as both weak and strong. Its challenge is not to determine whether I am strong or weak. To that question the only honest answer can be "Yes." We are, each of us, a blend of characteristic strengths and enduring weaknesses.

In Chapter Eight we explored the dual movement of conversion calling us to turn away from our sinfulness even as we become more tolerant of the weakness that remains. This image of strength in weakness is not unfamiliar to the Christian. The Gospels tell a story of strength and failure: Jesus' power to call us to pursue the Reign of God was not lessened by his inability to protect himself from death. "He was crucified through weakness, and still he lives now through the power of God" (2 Corinthians 13:4).

Saint Paul's letters explore and celebrate, with a special enthusiasm, the paradox of power and weakness in Christian life. At the end of his second letter to the Christians in Corinth, Paul reveals a personal difficulty: this strong, assertive minister was afflicted by "a thorn in the flesh." Troubled and humiliated by this weakness, he prayed to God to remove it from his life. But it did not disappear. In its enduring presence in his life, Paul sensed God's response: "'my power is at its best in weakness'" (2 Corinthians 12:9). Not "my power will overcome your weakness" or "my power is unconcerned with weakness," but "my power *is at its best* in weakness." This peculiar attitude toward personal weakness led Paul to say to those in Corinth, "I am quite content with my weaknesses . . . for it is when I am weak that I am strong" (12:10). If we are not quite content with our weaknesses, we can at least confirm, from our experience, that God seems to enjoy working through them. Often we accomplish things due to our abilities, and we give thanks. And not infrequently our abilities fail us; we are not strong enough to meet some challenge or problem. And yet, despite our failure, the problem or challenge is met. Nor is it that God skirts our weakness. Often enough, God's graceful results seem to arrive directly through our weakness.

We learn very gradually the Christian paradox of power. We are invited to grow strong and become virtuous, and we are called to befriend those enduring weaknesses that God sees fit to leave with us and through which God delights to act.

This paradox can help us heal some of the distress around power and leadership in the church. The leaders in the community of faith are not meant to be powerful, self-sufficient, without need. They are, in an ancient image, wounded healers. Ministry and healing are often provided by the weak in order, as we remember, to confound the strong. Leaders—and this makes them one with us and rescues them from a splendid isolation as "superiors"—are both strong and weak. Like any adult, they are gifted and flawed. This humanness of church leaders should remind us not to project idealized, impossible expectations on them. This humanness also invites us to reimagine leadership as a service *within* the community. Such a leadership, not isolated in its own power (and forced to conceal its weakness), will be able to take better advantage of the power and gifts available in the community. And the inequality of strengths in the group will not be a scandal but an invitation to mutuality—a sharing of power and weakness.

Reflective Exercises

Consider the experience of personal power in your own life by returning to the chart that appears on page 151.

1. Recall instances of your own power in each of these five different faces. Be as concrete as you can; think of particular events and situations of the past year or so. Spend time with these memories and the feelings that accompany them.

2. Which of these faces of personal power is most characteristic of you? Why do you think this is the case?

3. Which is least characteristic of you? Why is this so?

4. What change, if any, would you like to see in the balance among these expressions of power in your life right now?

Then take time to savor the paradox of "power through weakness" in your own life. First, recall a recent situation in which you were aware of God working through your weakness. Bring to mind again the people and circumstances and outcome. Then spend several moments in prayer, giving thanks for this special way in which the power of God moves through you.

12

Authority and Obedience

"And his teaching made a deep impression on them because, unlike the scribes, he taught them with authority" (Mark 1:22). Neither a priest nor a scholar, Jesus was an unlikely teacher in the religious hierarchy of his time. Yet here and elsewhere the Gospels report his assertive action: Jesus picks up the sacred texts in the synagogue and reads them with much force, "with authority." What is the source of this authority? How did he come by this convincing power? In a reflection on adult maturing we come eventually to the question of authority. What is authority, this bond that at once secures a human community and antagonizes it? What is the relationship of religious authority and the virtue of obedience?

Authority appears in our social life vested in various guises. Early encounters linger in our imaginations: parents, police, pastors. We begin life convinced that authority "belongs," naturally, to certain persons and special books and cherished traditions. Only gradually do we come to see our role in deciding who is in charge and determining what authority is to be obeyed.

Authority is an interpretation of power. Authorities—persons, laws, customs—arise from our judgments about power. We decide together, as a social group, which persons hold final responsibility in this organization, which of these ancient writings are the Word of God, which of these directives have the force of law. It is what we make of power among us that determines the shape of authority. To define authority as an interpretation of power is not to suggest that it is simply arbitrary and subjective, but it does remind us that we are participants in determining the pattern of authority in our civic and religious lives. We do not just "discover" the patterns of authority that we shall live by, we help decide them. More than children or victims, we are called to be partners in the social process of determining where power is among us and what uses of power are legitimate. We may be silent partners, reinforcing by our passivity a pattern that we hate. Or we may become active in the struggle to develop patterns more responsive to the common good. But we are always part of the interplay of social power that either reaffirms or challenges the current shape of authority.

If authority expresses our collective judgment about power, obedience is our response to these decisions. In obedience we pledge our fidelity to certain patterns of power and authority. Authority springs from a group's insights into power; obedience springs from our convictions that this authority is legitimate. Change occurs as we revise, as we see differently how power is among us; new insights shift our view of authority and invite a fresh obedience.

The complexity of authority is rooted in its special ambiguity. Social power moves in the dual directions of care and control. The power of our group nurtures us but also necessarily restrains us. Bonds of affection intersect with bonds of constraint. When restraint and oppression consistently overwhelm care and nurturance, social power comes under challenge. We enter a crisis of authority. In such a crisis, we sense that our accustomed way of understanding power among us is no longer fitting. This familiar face of social power is no longer friendly. Authority in this guise has become too much a mask. We begin to imagine, either in quiet reflection or in stormy revolution, a new face of authority. We search for a new image to describe the flow of power among us.

This process is at work today. We can obey only what we can first envision: God's presence in certain structures and styles of life; God's will as recognized in specific modes of community and personal behavior. In the church today, new visions of God's power among us call for the courage to "disbelieve" earlier images that, once graceful, no longer chart the movement of God. We struggle toward new images of authority and obedience that will more adequately express our fidelity to this movement. As we do so, we come to a renewed appreciation of both obedience and authority as virtues of Christian maturity. Each is a way of being powerful, each a way of being in touch with the power of God.

The Links Between Authority and Obedience

Authority and obedience are always interconnected. Both in defini-tion and in practice, they go together. In the social sciences, author-ity is defined as "the right to be heard and heeded," the right to be obeyed. Obedience, in turn, is "the proper response to legitimate authority." In practice, too, authority and obedience go together. Anyone who has been in a position of authority knows how bur-densome leadership becomes when it is not supported by willing colleagues. Where willing obedience is refused, authority is an empty claim. But willing obedience is mature only in response to legitimate authority. To set aside my own purposes or seriously modify my behavior for something less than legitimate authority is servility or simply cowardice.

Because authority and obedience are so linked, it is not sur-prising that their reputations rise and fall together. And both are under suspicion today. Many of us are unsatisfied with the models of authority we see in international relations, in corporate structures, even in personal life. Authority is so often authoritarian; obedience seems to demand subservience. In neither do we see the shape of mature behavior. In neither do we sense the strength of virtue.

But until somewhat recently, obedience was acknowledged among us as an adult strength. Citizens gave ready obedience to the laws of the land and to those in civil authority. The marriage cere-mony included the pledge to "love, honor, and obey." Religious women and men vowed obedience to the will of God made mani-fest through the will of the superior. But the value of obedience has declined among us. Today both obedience and authority seem to require justification.

Who among us can initiate action? Whose opinions do we take seriously? Ultimately, whose decisions prevail? These issues of ini-tiative and influence arise among us everywhere—in marriage, in the work place, in religious houses and ministry teams and diocesan commissions. The questions invite new answers today, answers that move beyond conventional understandings of who is "in charge." And there are efforts to fashion more mature models of obedience and authority. In religious houses we replace "superiors" with "coor-dinators." In families we work out roles that hold us mutually accountable. In the parish we move tentatively toward structures of shared decision making.

But in the midst of these efforts, many of us remain ill at ease. We have misgivings about turning away from former models of authority even as we are embarrassed by our allegiance to the structures that remain. As leaders, we feel awkward in the exercise of authority; as followers, we are cautious lest we be led astray . . . again.

If authority has suffered in the necessary process of reexamination, obedience has been under even more direct attack. There are the champions of autonomy who warn that any personal accommodation marks a move against integrity. In this view, to obey is to give up too much of myself. And there is some truth here: obedience makes demands on the self, as do love and friendship and teamwork. Each opens me to the demand for personal change. But in the process of change, each promises me more of myself as well. The demands for personal change that are a part of these "up close" relationships can lead me to greater self-possession as well as to my diminishment. If I defend against all personal change, I may avoid the risks that are part of obedience, but I avoid its maturing influence as well. And worse, I make a lonely choice. To avoid the demands of obedience, I may have to set myself outside the interplay of power, vision, and compromise that makes up so much of social life. Integrity demands flexibility more than self-defense. And the ability to obey, to accommodate myself for the purposes of a larger good, is integrity in one of its mature faces.

Our culture's commitment to individualism makes mature obedience suspect. But all of us who are attempting to sustain relationships of some depth—whether in marriage, ministry teams, or religious life—know how necessary is the strength of obedience. Without the willingness to modify personal behavior, it is difficult to deal with change as our relationship grows. Without flexibility, it is hard to respond creatively as our shared commitments take new shape. Without generosity, relationships remain at a superficial level that asks little of us. Without these resources of mature obedience, then, we are too fragile to face the demands of fidelity.

Accountability in Obedience and Authority

The social sciences remind us that neither authority nor obedience exists in isolation. They are, rather, aspects of group life, parts of the larger pattern of what goes on among us. Obedience and authority, then, can be discussed practically only in relation to a particular group—*this* marriage, *this* diocese, *this* corporation. Legitimate authority and mature obedience take shape *in this group* in terms of the common good, the shared purpose, the larger goal that the group holds or—perhaps more precisely—that holds the group.

Authority is the explicit face of social power. It is those patterns of initiative and influence that we understand to be legitimate. To "have" authority means to be acknowledged among us as having the right to be heard and heeded. This right may be based on a number of factors: the consent of the governed (in democracies), the divine right of kings (in medieval experience), lawful appointment (in bureaucracies), personal qualities of mind or heart (in many face-to-face relationships). But, ultimately, we acknowledge authority as legitimate—as having the right to make demands on us—because authority serves a larger good. The larger good that grounds the legitimacy of authority may be expressed differently, as "the common good" or "the goals of the group" or "the will of God."

Obedience is the voluntary accommodation of myself in the face of a larger good. I change my plans, I modify my behavior, I alter my goals. These accommodations are *obedient* when they are done in response to a purpose that goes beyond "just me." In society, we obey traffic laws in support of the larger good of public safety. In marriage, obedience enables us to do whatever is necessary to be faithful to the movement of our shared love. On a work team, we attempt to put private ambition at the service of the group effort. In the church, we struggle to stand—together—obedient to the Spirit, acknowledged as the sure and present guide of our common life. Obedience cannot be simple submission to the will or command of another person. Accommodation and submission are often required, but the focus of obedience is the larger good, to which we are all committed. It is this larger good that holds us all accountable.

This is the special accountability demanded in authority and obedience. No matter which role is ours in this interplay of social power, we can find ourselves called to an account. If I am in authority, I can be expected to explain my use of power; if I am obedient, I must be able to justify this as an adult act. Sometimes this accountability is expressed through the structures of management. In planning statements and budgets and annual reports, we give an account of our use of resources. But our mutual accountability must go deeper than management; we are called to an "account-ability." We must be able to give an account of our use of power, to tell the story of the larger purpose we serve and of our responsible actions in pursuit of this goal. This is the only way that the patterns of authority and obedience among us can be justified. This is the only path to virtue.

Neither authority nor obedience is good in itself. Each becomes legitimate among us by its connections with the larger good. This "larger good" is not a static goal. As we have seen in Chapter Two, if the group is alive, its sense of shared purpose—its deepest dream—is itself evolving. The sense of common purpose is never achieved in a fixed and final form. Theologian Bernard Loomer reminds us that "the common good is an emergent good." The structures of authority and obedience, then, are ultimately accountable to the shared dream, struggling to find form in planning meetings and budget decisions, taking shape in the messiness of conflict and collaboration, groaning to be born in our deepest and best hopes for our life together.

The Illusions of Authority

If authority arises from a vision of power among us, it is a vision easily distorted. Authority, as we are well aware, is a process prone to illusions. An illusion of authority is an image that no longer tells the truth; it is a portrait of social power that has become distorted. When such a distorted image becomes enshrined in public life, authority becomes, in theological terms, an idol. Christian maturity requires the constant breaking of idols, the continual purification of the illusions of authority.

A common illusion is that authority is a possession of the leader. This portrait of power imagines authority as an entity, a "thing" that someone owns. This picture hides the relational character of authority. As an interpretation of social power, authority is necessarily a reciprocal relationship; it expresses our agreement to be together. A leader or a set of rules receive authority from a group's agreement; a community's recognition of someone's right to lead makes this authority legitimate. Authority is the *bond* that holds this group together, not a private possession of a leader or a sacred text or a set of laws.

When authority is misunderstood as a private possession, another distortion follows: authority becomes unaccountable. If authority is "mine," something I hold independent of others, then I have no need to give an account of it to anyone. It is, precisely speaking, none of their business. I become an absolute authority. Power understood as a private possession produces absolute authorities; power understood as a social process in which we are all involved produces authorities who are accountable to the community.

A third illusion of authority distorts social power into privilege. Rather than a function of community service exercised in pursuit of the larger good, authority becomes a special status. The illusion nurtured here is that "the powerful" are different from the rest of us; it is on this difference that their privileged position among us depends. They are wiser or holier; they are physically stronger or have more direct access to God. Therefore their decisions and actions should not be questioned. In grateful acknowledgment of their superior gifts—which, so the illusion goes, are unavailable to the rest of us— we grant them obedience and the benefits that go with their office: status, wealth, social privilege. Authority becomes self-serving. The image of the leader here is not that of servant but of ruler.

Once authority is imagined as a personal and privileged possession, mutuality and accountability are forfeit. Mutuality is lost as the leader is set apart from those others who do not have power. When the leader is thus distinguished from "the rest of us," we are literally dispossessed of our own power. Leaders, with their power to rule, are not like us. They live on a higher plane or know secrets to which we have no access. Social analyst Elizabeth Janeway warns against this subtle tendency to "magical thinking" about our leaders. If our leaders are so unlike the rest of us, we may fear them or hate them or hold them in awe—but we cannot engage them as adult peers. Accountability is also abandoned. As a personal possession, the leader's authority does not come under the community's review. The leader may have to give an account to some superior but cannot be held responsible by the community that he or she heads.

Such distortions of authority spawn certain idols of obedience. Once authority is separated from the community, obedience becomes a virtue for followers only. The community's obedience is addressed to the leader and the system or ideology that the leader represents. Obedience is no longer a virtue of leadership. The leader is counseled to be honest and just—but not obedient. There is a crucial confusion here: the leader shifts from being seen as the *servant* of the larger good and becomes identified instead as the *object* of obedience. The result of this confusion, and often its goal, is that the process of social power is short-circuited. The energy of the group is diverted from the pursuit of its larger purposes. Authority and, especially, obedience are understood principally in terms of social control. Turned idol, obedience becomes a passive virtue. To obey means to be grateful and deferential and docile. The actions of Mahatma Gandhi and Martin Luther King challenge this idol and witness to a "disobedience" that safeguards a deeper obedience at its core.

Cultural Idols of Authority

In his provocative work *Authority,* social psychologist Richard Sennett shows how influential these illusions of authority have become. He points to two dominant but deficient images that serve to define leadership in Western culture today. The first of these is the paternal leader, who offers to care for us if we will but accept the price of (benign) control. This is an image of authority in which both power and maturity belong to the leader alone. The paternal leader wants to use these resources for the group but only according to the leader's idea of what is best—and only so long as the group recognizes and accepts its own impotence. There is no mutuality here. The group needs the leader (because the leader alone is imagined to have power), and the leader needs the group (to reinforce this image of unequal power), but the reciprocity of social power is denied.

Authority here is a static idol, with fixed categories of the powerful leader and the powerless group. The leader does not act in order to nurture the group's power but to substitute for it. Any movement of independent power within the group is interpreted as ingratitude (What more do you want from me?) or betrayal (After all I've done for you!). Paternalism is an authority of false love: where genuine love wants the continued growth of the beloved, paternalism wants continued dependence. This is an image of authority that confounds care and coercion.

A second influential image of authority is the autonomous leader. If paternalism is a mode of control that cares too much, autonomy is a mode that does not care. Here the leader is imaged as the disinterested expert. Perhaps the management consultant or the medical specialist or the government bureaucrat come to mind as examples of this kind of authority. Possessed of the resources of special competence or needed expertise, the leader-as-expert exercises this power in the group but asks nothing in return. At first glance, this can seem a liberating image of leadership. There are "no strings attached" to the power that the expert brings to the group. To those who know too well the strings that bind the group to a paternal leader, the image of the expert can seem a welcome alternative. But here again, the reciprocity of social power is denied. The group needs the power of the expert, while the expert has no need of the group. The image reflected is again that of unilateral power. In addition to the power of needed competence, the expert has the power of self-sufficiency. The emotional message "There is nothing I need from you" is most often interpreted as "You possess nothing of power or worth on your own."

In paternalism the implicit social equation is "You need me to care for you; I need you to be grateful." In autonomy it is "You need my expertise; I don't need you at all." Both these images are distortions: each seeks to establish an understanding of authority that denies mutuality. In each the process of power is one-way. In both paternalism and autonomy it is the leader who has power and choice. It is up to the leader to decide—when and if and how—to give this power to the group. In both these idols of authority the group stands outside the power that it needs: power is "without," outside the group. The group may be fortunate enough to benefit from the power of a leader. If so, it may make a return of gratitude, but lacking as it is in power on its own, it has nothing else to give. Even its gratitude is seen as less a choice than an expectation. For the group to expect more in its relationship to the leader is impertinence; besides, it will lead only to frustration. The group has nothing that the leader wants or needs. Its single stance is obedience, as the leader's single stance is authority.

The static quality of these two images is even more damaging. Neither expects—nor allows—the group's power to grow. Each image claims the current categories of leader and led are permanent.

Each predicts that any questioning of this status quo, the current balance of social power among us, can result only in chaos.

These two negative images influence patterns of authority in many institutional settings, but perhaps nowhere are the limits of paternalism being experienced as keenly as in the community of faith. In Chapter Four, for example, we pointed to paternalism as a factor that impedes the maturing of stewardship among us. The special urgency that surrounds the critique of paternalism in church life today invites us to explore this idol of authority in greater detail.

Paternalism—A Face of Authority

Under close scrutiny paternalism reveals an underlying tendency to confuse care and control. In paternalism the family experience of father and child is idealized and applied to other, larger groups in society. In the nineteenth century, paternalism was a social metaphor employed to soften the conditions of a burgeoning capitalism. The boss was presented not just as a taskmaster but as a father who cared for his worker-children. He would protect them, even house them; and, of course, he knew what was best for them because he had the perspective of the whole "corporate family."

The Christian community had much earlier adopted the image of fatherly care as a metaphor of its leadership. Family images were important in Christianity from its outset. The Gospels and epistles are rich in the language of family. Jesus prayed to God as his "Father," and his followers spontaneously imaged themselves as part of a family. As the church grew worldwide, it took on more bureaucratic structure. Even as this happened, the hierarchical model of the church—an organization marked by numerous strata, rankings, and laws—was softened by the complementary metaphor of Christians as a family. The international organization was imaged as "Holy Mother church"; its leader was known as "the Holy Father." Eventually the designated leader of each faith community, formerly named elder or presbyter, came to be called "father." Paternal care became a major metaphor of Christian ministry: priestly service was to be patterned on the care of God the Father for all his children. Paternal control evolved as a central image of church management: the local pastor and the bishop made their decisions with little consultation with the community.

In secular society and in the church, this face of authority provided clear benefits: a large group could envision its life as guided by the affection and concern of wise parents. The complex and sometimes harsh realities of social life could be imagined in more familial terms. The metaphor of paternalism, however, harbors powerful temptations, temptations to which both religious and secular authority have too often succumbed.

As a pattern of social behavior, paternalism is rarely overt or explicit. The boss does not announce that he is going to take care of you just like your father did, but the force of paternalism may be active just the same. We are likely to encounter paternalism in situations where we find ourselves in need. The need may arise in our work or in our political or religious life. In each case this need brings us to an authority figure who assures us he will "take care of it" for us. This authoritative person will provide for us, but in a fashion that demonstrates his control—of the situation and of us.

We are often uncomfortable in situations like this. Although our problem is taken care of, we experience a disconcerting array of emotions. Why am I so resentful? Why don't I feel grateful? Why do I feel belittled? Here is someone who has marshaled resources for my sake. But the feeling lingers: this was more an exercise of power than of care. Gradually I may begin to recognize the source of my discomfort. In this relationship I am not so much "cared for" as "taken care of." And I am made to feel indebted, bound to this authority figure not by mutual allegiance but by need.

We can recognize paternalism by its fruits. After such an encounter I am not more powerful, more capable of providing for myself the next time. Instead I have been momentarily provided for—and reminded of my childish status with this strong leader. I have not been empowered. I have been treated in a way that binds me in continuing dependence to this parental figure. I have been taken care of and diminished at the same time.

Paternalism is so difficult to confront because its practitioners are often unconscious of their behavior. Paternalistic leaders are likely to see only the care and not the control in their actions. They are both wounded and affronted at the suggestion of other motives behind their concern. To remove this mask of authority, we need a double discipline. We must clarify our own complex feelings of guilt, ingratitude, and impotence, and we must help leaders purify the motives that guide their exercise of power.

An Authority of False Love

The "ism" of paternalism warns us that this is a mode of authority gone awry. As Sennett observes, paternalism is "an authority of false love." His analysis of the distortions of authority involved in paternalism clearly illustrates the role of imagination in this metaphor gone wrong.

Three acts of the imagination are involved: selection, magnification, and distortion. In paternalism we select *one aspect* of a father for special attention: his care for his children. More precisely, we emphasize a father's guidance and supervision of his very small children. Second, this selected aspect of fathering is magnified: it is applied to a much larger social unit—a corporation or a church. This magnification itself leads to distortion at several levels. The factory of five hundred workers or the parish of nine hundred believers is not a family in the most basic sense, as a primary group. Such a large group does not enjoy the face-to-face intimacy of a family. Its members do not share the day-to-day tensions and delights of a family. Most of its members are adults rather than children.

The central distortion of paternalism, however, is the emphasis of one aspect of parenting to the neglect of others. Specifically, the paternalistic leader promises care but does not encourage the growth that would eventually launch the child as a free and independent adult. A single aspect of parenting—protective care—is isolated from other features and is thereby distorted. Sennett observes, "There is a promise of nurturance made in paternalistic ideologies, and the essential quality of nurturance is denied: that one's care will make another person grow stronger" (p. 82).

The image of the family in paternalism is of parents with very young children. In such a context, active parental control is necessary and good. But the distortion of the metaphor lies in its freezing of the family at this very early stage. As a family matures, the authority of the parents shifts. As parents we treat our eighteen-year-old differently than our eight-year-old. Children are included in family decisions in a different way as they move through adolescence toward early adulthood. A family that cannot make adjustments as its members mature will face a serious crisis. In a similar way, an organization that does not recognize—even encourage—the maturity of its members will suffer serious strain.

In these distortions of the image of the family, paternalism becomes a lie. Announcing its parental care, it employs this powerful metaphor for purposes of control. It not only "knows what is best"—what parent does not share this conviction?—it refuses to encourage growth. Paternalistic leaders need followers to remain children. Thus paternalism becomes a mask for domination. The guise of parental care disguises these purposes of control. This is what Sennett means in his description of paternalism as "an authority of false love."

Authority and Maturity

We manifest our maturity in our responses to authority—how we accept it and how we exercise it. It is easy to sense the immaturity of the adolescent who rejects every form of authority; no less immature is the adult who is too docile, who shows no inner sense of purpose. The maturing of authority can be charted along two lines. The first of these is the journey of authority inward.

We begin life with a necessary and near-total reliance on external power. As infants we cannot even feed ourselves; as children we are inducted into families and other communities that have developed rules and visions and boundaries. These external authorities guide our first steps of maturing.

The frequent trauma of adolescence and young adulthood centers on a conflict of authorities: How am I to follow the external rules of my family and society and still be obedient to the new ideas and hopes emerging within me? A common option at this early stage in the struggle for adult autonomy is to judge that I must abandon the influence of external authorities (parents, church, civic leaders) if the authority of my own life is to grow. The cultural ideal of individualism encourages this interpretation of authority in an "either/or" fashion: either the domination of external authority or the freedom of personal choice. Thus the first movements of personal authority are often tentative and defensive.

Fortunately, as we continue to grow we are delivered from this either/or dichotomy and drawn toward a balancing of authorities in our lives. The Christian sense of stewardship, which we explored in Chapter Four, enables me to combine my practical commitment to particular communities with confidence in my own vocation. Each is recognized as having its own authority; each demands an obedience and a fidelity. The midlife maturity that we have described as stewardship is itself an exercise of a complex authority: the authority of my personal calling is bonded to the authoritative convictions of our religious faith. The two dynamics that make this combination possible are mutuality and accountability. These dynamics also highlight the second movement of a maturing adult.

In a second shift of psychological and religious maturing, we "tip our world" from a vertical vision toward a more horizontal view. We begin to imagine the structure of human communities differently. Growing up, many of us picture the communities we live in—family, parish, city—in a vertical fashion. Authorities are located "above" others in this hierarchical world. Leaders stand over followers; leaders are meant to exercise authority, and followers are called to practice obedience. This simple world picture, which grows out of early family experiences and is reinforced by a social history of monarchy and other forms of hierarchy, tends to see authority as a possession of a leader—a possession likely to be permanent and even privileged. But as we mature, we become more conscious of the authority of our own lives. In so many of the important decisions with which we are faced, it is our own experience that must be heard and heeded. This new awareness of a complementary authority within us begins to tip our world: a vertical world of leader and led shifts toward a horizontal world of adult interaction. We are in this together. In our expectations of authority, mutuality begins to replace hierarchy. This does not mean that there are no differences among us or that no roles or offices are allowed. But we become aware that the roles and offices among us result from communal decisions and are meant to serve communal goals. Those designated as leaders among us remain members of the community. We are responsible to them as they are to us. As members of the community, leaders are accountable to the group and its vision and goals. We are no longer together only as parents and children or as rulers and followers. We are, at least in our most mature vision, partners in a shared enterprise. We are not always "equal" partners, because we each bring such different gifts and wounds. But we are mutual partners, because we recognize the need and strength that exists in each of us and acknowledge that our giving and receiving goes both ways.

As the route from the external authority of childhood to the balanced authority of adulthood is through the rugged terrain of adolescence, so it is with this shift in world visions. Commonly, a vertical and hierarchical view of authority does not tip gracefully toward a horizontal vision of an adult community. Instead the earlier world must be toppled. Rulers and parents and leaders of every type have to be dethroned. The religious name for this stage of adolescent change is anticlericalism. And, as our current experience in the church life confirms, this form of rebellion is not limited to those of us in our teens!

Fortunately, the dethroning of "fathers" and "superiors" is not a final goal but a route. On the other side of this purification awaits the new shape of mutual authority in an adult community of faith. To be sure, religious maturing can stall at the anticlerical phase as surely as psychological growth can be arrested in adolescence. Our complaints about priests and parents and other authorities, sustained too long, begin to look like an excuse for avoiding our own responsible participation in a community. Maturity is not the banishment of authority but its renewal and refigurement. This movement can both remove a privileged status from our leaders and welcome them into an adult community of mutuality and accountability.

The horizontal world envisioned here entails a blend of inner and outer authorities. We remain committed to the ideals of Christianity, but—as Jesus himself has counseled us—not as slaves but as intimates. As adults with particular gifts and unique vocations, we can allow the authority of our lives both to challenge and to be tested by the authority of our religious heritage. A well-developed flexibility has taught us that neither will crumble in this encounter. We are called to an obedience to both. Refusing an either-or choice, we invite the past and present to be mutually accountable to the shared ambition of the Kingdom of God. This vision of a future shaped by justice and love, a vision we neither invent nor fully possess, is the larger good that holds us as we seek, together, to obey and follow an elusive God.

Reflective Exercises

The goal of this reflection is to develop your own "working defini-tions" of authority and obedience.

1. Recall two or three recent occasions when you experienced someone exercising authority in a way that seemed to you to be legitimate. The person may be yourself or someone else; the sit-uations may be formal or informal. Take time with this initial step of recollection, noting three or four elements that seem important in each of the occasions you recall.
2. Compare your notes. What similarities and differences do you notice from one occasion to another?
3. Finally, write out three or four phrases that capture your sense of what is involved in legitimate authority. They need not be in the form of full sentences; words or examples may be sufficient.

Then repeat this process for a "working definition" of obedi-ence: recall several instances of mature obedience; note the ele-ments that seem important in each; compare them for similarities and differences; then work out three or four phrases that capture for you what is most important to mature obedience.

It can be instructive to do these exercises with a group of friends or colleagues and then to compare definitions. When this is done in an atmosphere of exploration and trust, much can be learned about the shape of authority and obedience today.

13

Women and Men
Together in the Church

An intriguing face of intimacy among us today is the experience of women and men working "up close" in the church. In some ways this is a new experience, at least in terms of our recent history as a religious people. From the beginning, both women and men have been centrally involved in Christian ministry. In recent centuries, though, ministry became increasingly understood in terms of specialized functions, with men and women less and less likely to be found working together. All this has changed dramatically over the past twenty-five years. One of the most far-reaching consequences of the renewal of communal life in the church sanctioned by Vatican Council II has been an explosion of ministry. With this has come a reunderstanding of how ministry happens in the community of faith. Classic distinctions of clergy and lay, of men and women, no longer segregate us from one another in ministry. There is a new immediacy in our dealings with one another. We work "up close." We are face-to-face, even if we don't always see things eye-to-eye.

This new interaction has proved to be a richly complex event, as relations among people usually are. Two aspects of this complexity are especially important for understanding the dynamics between women and men in work settings in the church today. These are the dynamics of attraction and of antagonism. Both of these have taken us by surprise.

Through the late 1960s and into the 1970s, the "problem" of which we were most aware was attraction: How are we to deal responsibly with the affection, even romance, that can develop between men and women who work together? Over the last ten years the shape of the problem has changed. Now when we discuss the "problem" of women and men working together it is usually not attraction we are talking about; it is hostility.

Affection and hostility are normal ingredients of interaction between people. When we come "up close," many emotions are generated, frequently strong emotions, sometimes even conflicting emotions. That we should experience these dynamics toward one another in our shared ministry is to be expected, even to be enjoyed. We can predict that both attraction and antagonism will continue to enliven our ministry teams and work groups in the future. But it is on the experience of hostility between women and men in ministry today that we will focus here, examining some of the underlying factors that seem to be involved.

Some experience of hostility among coworkers and colleagues is inevitable. In the course of dealing with one another we get in each other's way, we offend each other's sensitivities, we take each other for granted, we let each other down. It is part of the human condition. These misunderstandings and mistakes require of us patience, forbearance, forgiveness. Most of us understand this strain as normal and accept it as a part of the process of working with others. But the hostility between men and women in the church today seems somehow to go beyond this expectable strain. There often seems to be more conflict than can be explained by the evidence at hand. It is the dynamics of this "more" that we want to examine here.

As we start we must acknowledge that the elements underlying the hostility between women and men in the church today are complicated. Our discussion here will not do justice to them all. We will consider only two factors that may be at play. One is a question of developmental maturity, the other an issue of social change. Each is relevant to both women and men: factors of developmental maturity will influence the way that both women and men deal with each other; both men and women are influenced by larger forces of social change. But there is evidence to suggest that the developmental issue we are considering is especially pertinent for many men, as the social issue we will discuss is especially influential for many women. So, aware of the risk of oversimplification involved, we will speak of the *developmental issue* as underlying some of the hostility that men in ministry may feel toward women, and the *social issue* as explaining some of the antagonism that many women in ministry experience toward men.

The Developmental Issue—Women as Other

Developmental psychology examines the normal processes of growth and maturity across the life span. An important moment in this process occurs in adolescence as the young person moves toward an initial adult sense of self. Important in this sense of self is an awareness of gender identity—that I am a woman or that I am a man. Psychologists do not yet understand all that is involved in this process of adolescent gender identity, but we are aware of some of the important factors.

One of these factors is a dynamic of distancing. In a first step, as it were, in the process of understanding "who I am" as an adult male, the adolescent boy sets himself apart from those who are "not male." Women are experienced as "not me," as "other." In most cases this process is quite normal, a natural part of an important maturational event. We can see evidence of this even before adolescence—the nine-year-old who refuses to join the neighborhood softball team because "they're letting the girls play!"

In adolescence the process becomes more complex. By the early teens, the physical and psychological changes of puberty have called into question many elements of the young person's earlier sense of self. Sex and sexuality become increasingly important in a new understanding of who I am and, especially, who I am not. At this point the normal adolescent process of distancing myself from women in order that I may identify myself as a man focuses especially on sex. Women are other than me, and it is especially in regard to their sexuality that they are other. Again, all this is normal and expectable. (And, it may be useful to recall, a comparable dynamic of gender identification is going on among adolescent women.)

For some adolescent males, however, the process is yet more complicated. These young men experience women not only as sexually "other" but as dangerous. I am aware that women—girls—are involved in these powerful new impulses of sexuality within me, over which I often sense I have little agency. I experience myself as subject to feelings and desires that somehow "they" seem to provoke, sometimes without my consent, often even beyond my control. Surely "they" are dangerous to me in their scary sexual power.

So the process of coming to identify oneself as an adult man often involves a profound experience of women as "other," as "other" primarily in their sexuality, and—at least for some men—as dangerous because of this sexuality.

This dynamic seems to be a quite normal part of adolescent development. And most of us know this. We sense that while the process can obviously complicate a teenager's life and times, it's not a bad way to be fifteen. But it's an awkward way to be thirty-five! To be in one's thirties and *still* relate to women primarily as "other" and dangerous is to be seriously limited in the ability to live and work in the adult world.

How, then, does the young man get beyond this "normal" adolescent experience of distancing to that point where he is able to relate to women in a more adult manner? There are, to be sure, many ways in which this important personal journey is made. We look here at two of the typical paths.

For some, overcoming the early sense of polarity between men and women or, more precisely, between *me* and women, comes as a benefit of an experience of love in adolescence. This romance brings me into relationship with one woman, this particular girl with whom I am in love. If the relationship lasts long enough (and, since it is an early experience of love, this "long enough" usually does not mean "forever"), it can bring me beyond the initial experience of sexual fascination and romance to the point where I experience *this girl* in her individuality. As this happens I gradually come to an appreciation that she is more like me as a human being than she is "other," as a representative of that alien category "women."

This relationship thus introduces me into an experience of women as "like me," at least potentially.

It is not always romance that invites a young man beyond an early stereotyped emotional response to women. For some, the transformation happens through personal experience with a variety of women. In his job, in his family, in his social contacts, he experiences different kinds of relationships with a number of different women. These experiences bring him to the realization that women are very diverse among themselves, as are men. Some he likes and others he does not. Some are different from him in their attitudes and experiences, but many see things very much as he does. Some are sexually attractive to him and some are not. Some are hostile and alien and dangerous to him, but most are simply persons trying to make their way in life, just as he is.

The ability to be aware of women as persons (rather than just as sexual entities) and to experience them as individuals (rather than just as representatives of the category "women") is basic for an adult relationship between women and men. It should not come as news that not all men have achieved this adult stance. There are many men in American society—married and single, clergy and lay—for whom women are still a univocal group, even an alien category. It is difficult for these men to experience a particular woman as *this person*. They are more likely to respond to her as "one of them." And the category of "them" is defined overwhelmingly in sexual terms.

For some men, then, it is this sexual category to which she belongs that defines *this woman*. Nothing else about her is important enough to register in the relationship. Because they see her basically in sexual terms, some of these men will be titillated by her—even aside from any behavior on her part—because that is the way they experience those who are part of the category "women." But others will be frightened of her—again, even apart from her actual behavior—for the same reason: because she falls in that dangerous category of sexually "other." Some men display this fear of women openly, but in others it is masked. Fear, after all, is not a very "manly" emotion—fear of women even less so. So in some men, the negative emotional response they feel—their fear of women as somehow dangerous—is expressed (and sometimes even experienced) as hostility.

What does all this have to do with ministry? It is our contention that some of the conflict experienced between women and men in ministry today is related to this hostility. This is not to say that most men in ministry are hostile toward women. Nor is it to suggest that most have not moved into an adult psychological stance in their relationships with women. But it is to point out that there are a number of men—married and single, clergy and lay—of whom these two statements are true. And there are factors in our recent history as a religious group that have made the situation somewhat more complicated for Catholic ministers.

The preparation for ministry that most priests and men religious receive has, until quite recently, been influenced by an understanding of celibate lifestyle that has made mature relationships with women difficult for them to achieve. This does not mean that celibacy is necessarily a barrier to personal maturity. Our church has too long been enriched by the lives and witness of mature celibate men and women for us to give credence to that claim. But we are aware today that there are elements in the celibate *lifestyle*—especially as it was understood prior to Vatican Council II—that have made it difficult for celibate men to move beyond a less mature range of attitudes and behaviors toward women. Many celibates have, nevertheless, matured in their capacity to relate to women, but often they attest that this has been in spite of rather than because of the prevailing expectations of the celibate culture.

Until quite recently, for example, brothers and priests began their formal training at the beginning or end of high school—at a time when, normally and expectably, they would be involved in an early stage in the process of gender identification. Normally and expectably, then, we can anticipate that many of these young men began their religious training with the experience of women as "other," as primarily sexual beings who are vaguely "dangerous" to oneself. The all-male living arrangement into which they entered provided little opportunity to deal with a variety of women (one of the ways in which men their age might come to a more mature awareness of women). There was little opportunity and certainly no encouragement for the development of a romance or other emotionally significant relationship with a woman (another route open to other men their age). In some seminaries and novitiates, the dominant ideology reinforced the negative image of women as exclusively sexual creatures, dangerous to one's vocation and detrimental to one's ministry. It is not surprising, then, that many men completed their early training without significant advancement beyond an adolescent stance toward women.

The movement into active ministry did not automatically move the process ahead. The proscriptions of the celibate lifestyle were clear in regard to women. The priest's living arrangements and, to a large extent, work setting were still almost exclusively male. He was warned against spending any more time with women than absolutely necessary for his ministry; he was enjoined not to be seen alone with a woman in public. Any activity that could be interpreted as deviating from these norms would be sure to incur the disapproval of his peers and, if public, to cause scandal among the flock.

It is not surprising, then, that a number of religious men have not had the kind and quality of relationships with women necessary to ground an adult interpersonal stance. Equally, it is not surprising that many of these men characteristically choose to avoid dealing with women whenever possible. But the avoidance of women is becoming less and less possible! Laywomen are increasingly active in the life and ministry of the church and, following the lead of women religious, are assuming more visible roles of leadership in the community of faith. More and more, celibate men are engaged not only in ministry *to* women but in ministry *with* women, as colleagues and coworkers. This expansion of ministry has been a boon for the church and an enrichment for ministers, as most of the men and women involved are willing to attest. But for some men the new shape of ministry has forced them into ongoing relationships for which they feel unprepared. Worse, they feel afraid. Often this fear is expressed as defensiveness, as anger, as suspicion. The women involved are often at a loss to explain the hostility they feel directed at them. Efforts to determine the cause of the problem seem not to avail; attempts to negotiate a solution seem only to make things worse. The problem, of course, is that "the problem" is not what it seems. It is not what she is doing that generates the hostility; it is who she is—a woman.

Some of the conflict that exists today between men and women in ministry is related to this issue of developmental maturity. When we see a level of hostility that seems to go beyond the evidence at hand, its source may be in part a defensiveness toward *women* (as a category) that makes it difficult for a man to deal with *this* woman, who is now functioning "up close" in ministry.

The Social Issue—
Changing Women's Consciousness

But clearly, not all conflict between men and women can be explained in developmental terms. If this issue helps us understand a dynamic of hostility that influences some men, there are other factors that seem more influential among women in ministry today. Particularly important is the social experience of a changing consciousness among women. Here again, both men and women are affected by this social phenomenon. But it is the effect of this changing consciousness on women that will concern us here.

There is virtually no woman active in ministry today, and probably few even among the less active members of our parishes, who has not been influenced by the movement for women's liberation. This is not to say that most women in the church identify themselves as feminists—Christian or otherwise. This is simply not so, at least not at this time. Nor does this mean that most women are in agreement on the issues and strategies involved in "women's issues." As anyone who has been close to the issues knows, the range of responses among women is as great as that among men. To say that every woman has been influenced, then, is rather to remind us that every woman has had to deal with the issues—in her own mind if not in public. Women today (and men, to be sure) are continually confronted with the conflicting ideologies and the contradictory "facts" that are part of this movement of social change. Many women have had to take a stand in some way or another, even as they remain aware of how their sense of what is the right stand to take for themselves and for the movement tends to shift.

For most women, their involvement—however modest—in the larger social process of reunderstanding the role of women has dramatic consequences in their understanding of themselves. It is this process of changing consciousness that we will examine here, especially as it influences relations between women and men. We will turn to the research being done today regarding the development of moral consciousness for clues to assist us.

In a provocative analysis of changing black consciousness, James Fowler has discussed an expectable process of moral commitment in persons whose lives have been caught up in the dynamics of social change. We will draw on Fowler's analysis in our discussion here, applying it to the experience of women.

There is a pattern that emerges in the process of personal transformation that accompanies social change. The moments or stages in this process are marked by a differing sense of self. When they are first confronted with "women's issues," many women are at a stage of *conventional thinking*. At this stage, a woman experiences congruence between her own experience and the culture's definitions of what it is to be a woman. What her culture says women are, she senses that she is. The culture's expectations of a woman's life express what she hopes for her own. The generally accepted description of a "good woman" reflects the norms by which she judges her own conduct. When there is disparity between this image of the "good woman" and her own behavior, she holds herself accountable. Even if she is not to blame (if, for example, there are extenuating circumstances that explain and excuse her behavior) she will most often still feel somewhat guilty for falling short of this cultural image of how a woman should act.

An example may help here. Sister Agatha has been the religious education coordinator in Holy Name Parish for the past seven years. She is a woman in her fifties who spent almost twenty years teaching in elementary schools before she moved into parish-based ministry. Her work at Holy Name has met with a good deal of success. In her seven years the program has developed from one course she taught after school for the confirmation class to a parish-wide ministry of religious education staffed by parishioners themselves. She has organized a network of adult volunteers committed to their own religious development and available for service to others in the parish.

Toward the end of May the pastor calls Sister Agatha to his office for a conference. He has good news, he tells her. He has just learned that one of the newly ordained priests will be assigned to Holy Name, arriving sometime in July while she is away on retreat. Sister Agatha is thrilled. There has been need of another priest in the parish for a long time. A young priest should be a fine witness to the teens and young adults. She will look forward to meeting him when she returns to the parish in the fall. "And another thing," the pastor continues, "young Father Bob wants to take over the parish religious education program as part of his ministry. He took an education course in the seminary, and his professor said he did a very good job."

At the stage of conventional thinking, Sister Agatha may feel some disappointment at this announcement, but she is not likely to sense that any injustice has been done. After all, what are sisters for but to take up the work of ministry when there are not enough priests to go around? Now that a priest is available, it is her role to help him move into the job she previously occupied and then to step aside gracefully. She will keep her disappointment to herself and turn her gaze toward other work that needs to be done. Now, without the responsibility for coordinating the religious education volunteers, she can give her energy to developing a program for visiting shut-ins in the parish.

In this example, then, there is congruence between Sister Agatha's sense of herself and her culture's definitions of what a woman is, especially what a woman religious is. There is no problem here for Sister Agatha; at this stage of conventional thinking, she experiences the world working as it is supposed to.

But not all women would respond as did Sister Agatha! More and more women are no longer at the stage of conventional thinking. They sense not congruence but discrepancy between their own experience and the norms and expectations that dominate the culture. They have moved to a new place in the process of self-understanding. And for many this movement brings them into a stage of *dichotomous thinking*. The movement away from conventional thinking is often gradual. A woman slowly comes to sense that her experience of herself does not fit "the way things are supposed to be." Initially she may judge that *she* is the problem and try to modify herself so that she "fits" once again. But as her experience of her "differentness" grows, she may well begin to question not herself but the cultural definitions that no longer fit. Her experience has given the lie to the norms and expectations of conventional thinking. She may feel she has been misled, even betrayed. Now wary of the culture's images of "how things are," she must develop new criteria for interpreting and evaluating her world. And it is often the criteria of dichotomous thinking that emerge at this stage.

In dichotomous thinking, the world is perceived in terms of opposites: good and bad, friend and enemy, female and male. At this point some women experience men—*all* men—as the enemy. Newly aware of the many ways in which women are oppressed, they are alert to oppression everywhere. Now conscious of the hidden faces of discrimination, they have become suspicious of motives and gestures and behavior that previously were of little concern. They see chauvinism everywhere—in part because it *is* so widespread, in part because of their new sensitivity.

It is difficult to be in the dichotomous stage—difficult for women, difficult for the men in their lives. Women in the dichotomous stage feel much anger: against the culture that has lied to them, against the institutions that have failed them, against the norms that continue to constrain them, and—often—against the men with whom they live and work. A good deal of the anger that women experience is justified in the evidence of discrimination at hand. But women in the dichotomous stage often experience an anger that goes beyond the evidence.

Take the experience of Millicent. A married woman and mother in her thirties, Milly has recently become more involved in parish life. Two years ago she allowed her name to be put forward for the parish council and, to her delight and surprise, she was elected to a three-year term. The experience on the council has been important for her. She has proved herself one of the most capable council members and was named by her peers to the executive committee. Among the committee's responsibilities is preparing the agenda for the monthly council meetings. Milly has always enjoyed the executive committee meetings. The group is small—just two men, two other women, and herself. They work well together and enjoy each other's company, too. Milly has always loved to cook. About a year ago she started bringing some little home-baked delight to each executive committee meeting for the group to share over coffee together when its work was done. The other members have been quite appreciative, both of her thoughtfulness and of her skill as a cook.

As is the case in many parishes, the council does not meet over the summer months, so neither does the executive committee. As a treat for herself over the summer, Milly decides to take a theology course offered at the local Catholic college. Eager to know more about the Scriptures, she registers for "Women and the Bible." The course is taught by one of the most highly respected professors at the college, a woman religious who identifies herself at the first class as a committed Christian feminist. For Milly the course is an eye-opener.

Early in September, as her family is leaving Sunday Mass, Milly is approached by Tom Foster, the president of the parish council and one of Milly's fellow members on the executive committee. Tom is checking with her to find a convenient date for the first committee meeting of the season. As he turns to rejoin his family, Tom calls back to Milly, "Be sure you bring one of those great blueberry coffee cakes this time!" Milly fixes him with a steely stare and says back to him, "What do you mean, 'Be sure to bring a coffee cake!' That's just the problem in this parish. All we women are seen as good for is the cooking and the cleaning. If you want coffee cake at the meeting, then you bring coffee cake. That's not what I'm on the committee for!"

The example is an exaggeration, to be sure, but it is not too far off the mark. Where did Milly's anger come from? She is probably asking herself that question. Tom is a friend; he has been very supportive of her activities in the committee and is her staunch ally in the larger parish council. Yet her new awareness of the ways that women *have* been treated and still *can* be treated has changed her perception of even the apparently "innocent" conventions of social life.

Milly's anger may seem excessive, at least in this example, but it is not without its value. For many women, anger is an important spur to the movement beyond conventional thinking. It is not easy to stand against the accepted norms and conventions of one's culture. There are many pressures, both from within and from without, to accept these cultural images as definitive and to conform one's experience to them. Where does a woman get the strength to stand with her experience, apart from the prevailing cultural norms? Some of the strength she needs comes from her anger.

But, granting that this anger can be useful, it is seldom easy. It is not easy for the woman, who finds herself angry so much of the time; it is not easy on the men who are part of her life, because often the anger is directed at them. How does a woman continue the process of transformation? Where does she go from the stage of dichotomous thinking?

It must first be noted that not all women move beyond this point. For some, the sharp distinctions of dichotomous thinking continue to describe the world of their experience; the clear categories of good and evil continue to separate women from men. But many women report that another important shift in self-understanding has been part of their own journey. Using a term from developmental theory, we can speak of this shift as a movement into a stage of *integrated thinking*. As a woman makes this move, she does not leave her anger behind. Anger, as we saw in Chapter Nine, is an important adult emotion, appropriate in many situations. And the signs of injustice and oppression which generate much of her anger still remain. But her experience of anger now is accompanied by more control. In the dichotomy stage, women often report that they feel overwhelmed by their hostility; it is their anger that is in control. Now anger continues as a frequent companion, but there are more choices available for handling their anger. They can be more objective in their anger, evaluating the feelings of hostility that arise and attempting to determine their cause and their proper object. They can decide whether—and when—and how to express anger. Thus anger, often an alien emotion for a woman, can be accepted as part of herself and can become an important resource in her continuing commitment to social change.

This stage is integrative in that a woman can incorporate this anger, can integrate it into a larger sense of a responsible self. It is integrative in the social sphere as well. In the dichotomous stage a woman is likely to recognize men as "the enemy," sensing that some male action or inaction is responsible for the injustices that she and other women experience. And this perception is often accurate! But in dichotomous thinking, this "them against us" attitude can prevail to such an extent that it overwhelms evidence to the contrary. *All* men are suspect; their support is discounted as patronizing, their critique is dismissed as typical male animosity. At the integrative stage, a woman's judgments become more nuanced. Yes, there are men who are the enemies of women, but there are men who are their friends and supporters as well. In her own life she can recognize not only those men who have thwarted and perhaps even injured her; but she can also recognize those who have called her to life and celebrate those who have championed her cause. She comes to realize that the line that divides good and evil does not neatly separate women from men. Rather it cuts through the heart of each person, even herself. She is then able to acknowledge her own ambivalence and appreciate the ways in which she has been a part of her own oppression. She wants to be accepted as a responsible adult and treated as a person in charge of her own life. But it is tempting to let other people make the really difficult decisions and thus avoid the possibility of making a mistake herself. She resents being treated as a sex object, but a little flirting now and then sure is fun.

The Consequences for Ministry

What does all this have to do with ministry? Women in the church today range all along this process of reunderstanding themselves and their role in the community of faith. As more and more move beyond the categories and convictions of conventional thinking, we can expect an increase in anger among us. Some of the conflict experienced between women and men in ministry, then, finds its origin here. Women, both religious and lay, are increasingly sensitive to the evidence of injustice and increasingly outspoken in their opposition to its presence in the church and in society. At times this outspokenness will include confrontation, with the anger and hostility that can attend. This is in itself a new experience of conflict among us. But there is more involved. Some of these women are at the dichotomous stage, their anger seeming to "go beyond" what the situation demands. As we saw above, this anger can be an important part of a movement of personal transformation, but it is anger nevertheless. It is likely to generate the responses that strong anger evokes—hurt feelings, defensiveness, withdrawal, more anger in return. And this has happened among us, in our parishes and ministry teams and offices and schools.

The French existentialist Jean Paul Sartre wrote in his play *No Exit* that "hell is other people." A sentiment closer to the experience of many of us in ministry these days may be that hell is a ministry staff that is composed of men who are afraid of women as sexually "other" and women who are at the stage of dichotomous thinking. This painful picture does not describe most ministry teams or diocesan commissions or parish committees; for that we can be grateful. But it is frequent enough in the experience of the church today to invite our serious attention.

In a time of tension and conflict we can be consoled by an important insight: as a people we have done this to ourselves; we can undo it. For centuries we have structured a severe distance between women and men. We have exaggerated the dangers and antagonisms that are a necessary part of Christian intimacy and ministry. This crisis in contemporary church life may be imagined not as a hell but as an opportunity and invitation. Men in ministry can mature beyond a defensiveness that sees women as sexual dangers or as ministerial intruders. Women in ministry can move toward a recognition of men not as an oppressive category but as an assemblage of diverse persons, expectably both gifted and wounded.

A new, more mature face of intimacy is appearing in Christian ministry today. The hoary ideal of the self-sufficient minister is giving way to visions of a shared ministry. We are beginning to witness practically to what we have always preached—that Christian communities are graced in surprising ways with a variety of ministerial gifts and that in this work of the Lord we have deep need of one another.

Reflective Exercises

Recall the different settings in which you have experienced women and men "up close" in the life of the church—in ministry, in friendship, in worship. Spend time with these memories of the situations, the people involved, your own participation. Then consider these questions:

1. In your own experience, what are the benefits of collaboration between men and women—benefits to you, to others, to ministry, to the church?
2. What are the problems that you have experienced in these settings, the tensions or difficulties or concerns?
3. What "works"? What factors well support the efforts of women and men to be together in the life of the church today?

14

Generous Absence

This book has been concerned with presence: God's presence to us in our vocations; the presence in our life of imagination and of anger; the presence of women and men to one another in the church. But a concern for presence must include an interest in absence. Absence is not simply the lack of presence; absence itself is often a mellow mode of being present. This peculiar aspect of absence is explored in this final reflection on Christian maturing.

Christian spirituality is rooted in the experience of presence. Jews and Christians trace their origins to Abraham's awareness of the presence of someone urging him to leave home and pursue a new way of life. His descendants, wandering in the Sinai Desert hundreds of years later, also sensed a presence—some power lurking among them, giving a certain direction to their journey. Before our God had a name (Yahweh) or a face (allowing us to call God "Father"), this force was known simply as "presence"; in Hebrew, *Shekinah*. In their daily encampments and at Mount Sinai our ancestors came in touch with this mysterious presence.

Contemporary Christians experience this presence in similarly murky but compelling ways: we sense a certain direction that our lives should follow; we are drawn toward specific commitments of love and work. Yet for a number of Christians today this basic experience of presence has been lost. "The presence of God" has become little more than a pious phrase. In the long history of our attempts to come into this presence, we have at times been tempted to romanticize it. Some devotional accounts of the lives of the saints, for example, seem to suggest that "really holy" Christians enjoy a clear and enduring awareness of God in their lives. This portrait, meant as an ideal but often becoming in practice a distortion, leaves many of us with a sense of inferiority. "If *that* is what God's presence means, my faith is pretty shabby." For those of us who share this sense of distance from the "ideal," it can be useful to recall our religious ancestors' sense of presence.

A Desert Presence

The Yahweh that Moses followed was revealed as a desert presence. It was not the radiant presence of a king on a throne, nor of a Lord in the temple. It was most often a presence in the midst of absence. Moses and his people recognized God's power in the burning bush. They came upon manna and saw it as a clue to a caring presence. Setting up a special tent at the edge of their camp, they would await the visitation of this power. Sometimes it would come, appearing in the rustling of the wind. At other times there was no movement in the tent, no sense of someone present. This was a "sometimes presence."

This presence in absence, this "sometimes" awareness, strikes a deep chord in many Christians today. Our own religious maturing happens often enough in this context: we get wind of God's presence in an inhospitable desert. In such an environment faith is sustained by finding traces and hints and scents that remind us of a benevolent presence. And absence is not just the context of this presence; it is often the very mood in which God's presence is felt.

The liturgical reform of the 1960s was an important step in this recovery of a lively sense of absence. As worshiping Catholics, we had, it seemed, become saturated with presence: our altars were filled not only with God's enduring presence in the tabernacle but with other signs of presence—crucifixes, candles, relics, and statues on every side. Christ's presence was emphatically celebrated in the ceremony of benediction, where we could "see" this presence in the monstrance. As a believing people we were steeped in presence. The liturgical reform, so traumatic for some of us, reasserted absence as the environment of God's presence. The altar, turned toward the people, was emptied of its tabernacle; the sanctuary was simplified; some statues were removed. The devotion of benediction was celebrated rarely.

We deprived ourselves of these signs of presence, seemingly drawn by a need for absence: we were clearing space, making room for something. Some of us mourned the loss of these signs of presence; others felt we were lapsing into Protestantism with its "empty churches." Many Catholics also had a feeling of freedom. It was not so much a freedom from past liturgical practices but a freedom for more fitting celebrations of God's presence. It was a freedom of absence. As a people we are being attracted again to the deeply traditional connections between absence and faith.

The Trauma of Absence

The experience of absence can be friendly, a companion of freedom. But it most often is experienced in trauma. Absence comes as loss, as failure and death. One example may stand for our many different encounters with traumatic absence.

A dear friend, a woman religious in her mid-thirties, recently lost her father. His death happened at a time in her life when she was already struggling with change and loss. This sudden loss precipitated yet another: she came to realize that she had lost her faith. She could no longer believe in a God who would deprive her of her father. With his death ensued a profound absence of God in her life. Her friends and colleagues struggled to honor this absence—to acknowledge her loss of faith while surrounding her with their own. For a time, in the absence of her faith, her friends and community believed for her. Respecting this important absence, they also surrounded her with the presence of their own faith. And with time (this is an ancient story, relived endlessly in our religious heritage) a new faith began to replace the absence in her heart. A tougher, more adult faith very gradually took root in this empty space. An earlier faith, inadequate for her new experience, had fallen into the ground and died. Deprivation and absence were the soil in which a new, more robust faith began to grow.

The more we share our stories of belief (and unbelief), the more we come across this too-well-kept secret: our faith communities always include people who are losing their faith. A common way for hardier, more adult faith to come to life is through death—the loss of a style of faith that is too adolescent, too narrow to fit the demands of the future.

This expectable and ordinary role of absence in our faith life becomes clearer as we better understand the dynamic of adult crises. In a crisis—whether this is the death of a loved one, the loss of a job, or the experience of divorce—I undergo disorientation and loss. Some important part of myself, of my life, is being taken away from me. Initially I may resist with every type of strategy and distraction, but if I am fortunate, I learn to let go. And in the letting go, in the deprivation and absence this allows, I create space for the next stage of my life. Mourning my loss, I gradually absent myself from what I had deemed essential. Very often, in this absence (this desert of the crisis), unsuspected strengths appear, unexpected possibilities emerge. In this absence—if I am still enough and graced enough— I experience something or someone inviting me in new directions.

These crises appear in life not simply because we are sinful or immature, but because this is how we grow. It is a dynamic that should not be too alien to the believing Christian: by losing myself, I gain myself; by dying to some cherished or accustomed part of my life, the next stage of life is born. And at the center of this dynamic stands absence. Absence is often the desert environment of God's presence and the path that religious maturing follows.

A Tradition of Absence

Between the Sinai Desert and the contemporary experience of crisis, our Christian tradition is richer with absence than we may have noticed. Perhaps it is embarrassment about this absence that has led us to ignore it. One small but significant example of such embarrassment occurs in the liturgical reading for the Second Sunday after the Epiphany. This reading celebrates the Judeo-Christian conviction about personal vocations by recalling the story of Samuel being called by God (1 Samuel 3). This story of a vocation is, of course, about presence—Samuel's sense of Yahweh's presence in his life as he hears a voice repeatedly calling "Samuel, Samuel!" But in this reading, the first verse of the scriptural story is omitted, perhaps because it observes that "it was rare for Yahweh to speak in those days; visions were uncommon" (3:1). This historical context of God's absence, which makes the call to Samuel even more dramatic, may have been judged to be catechetically embarrassing, and so was omitted. Whatever the motivation, such an editing of this story distracts us from the context of Samuel's vocation, and many others' as well.

The experience of absence also stands at the very center of the Christian faith. In his passion and death Jesus Christ reveals the power of absence in several ways. Mark's Gospel recalls that at the approach of his death, Jesus felt a terrifying absence: "'My God, my God, why have you deserted me?'" (Mark 15:34). The only Son of God, at the point of death, feels the utter absence of God.

From the beginning of our tradition, we have been uncomfortable with such stark absence and have attempted to soften it in various ways. The writer of the fourth Gospel, so struck by Jesus Christ as the transcendent Word of God, the Son of God in perfect union with his Father, could not remember that final saying; it does not appear in John's Gospel.

In the midst of this sense of abandonment, Jesus prays, "'Father, into your hands I commit my spirit'" (Luke 22:46). The presence of God survives, if barely, in a desert of absence.

But Jesus' death was also an experience of absence for his followers. In his death they (and we) lost their leader; where there had been the Lord, there was now absence. This absence of Christ from the Christian community is celebrated in the Ascension. This was not the absence of God, because our loss of Jesus meant the coming of the Spirit. But our belief in the second coming of Christ means that his absence is real. To fully believe in the second coming we must believe in Jesus' absence. And we must honor this absence.

Absence as Generous

Jesus Christ, we believe, came to give life. Both his life and his death generated more life. His life was "generous" in the fullest sense: it gave us something extraordinary. How was his death, this enormous loss, a generous absence?

Out of Jesus' life and death was generated the Christian community. In his life he showed us how to live, and in his death he created space for our leadership. Jesus' death was an emptying and an abnegation that generated our adult responsibility and authority. As long as he was present among us, we could be content as followers, as disciples of a present Lord. But in his absence a vacuum was generated, an empty space into which first the Apostles and

Paul, then subsequent generations of Christians, would step. The absence of Christ is the context of the style of Christian maturity and leadership that we explored in Chapter Four as stewardship.

In Jesus' absence the early Christian communities had to make important decisions about their faith life. No longer able to simply ask the Lord (an action proper to a disciple), they now had to rely both on their memory of Jesus and their own best instincts of what was the most faithful decision. But the decision, made amid debate and conflict, was theirs. Thus was stewardship—that frightening but unavoidable experience of responsibility and authority—born in the church.

The New Testament argues for an intimate connection between stewardship and absence. In the well-known parable of the faithful steward in Luke's Gospel (chapter 12), we find that the context of the steward's virtuous activity is the master's absence. It is while the owner is away that the steward must make responsible decisions about the household. This absence of the Lord is, in fact, a special mode of Christ's presence. Christ remains among us—not to provide clear answers but to encourage us to responsible and courageous decisions. He is present in our communities but not as an authority that substitutes for our adulthood, which would leave us as children. It is a presence that compels us to participate in the building up and purifying of our communities. But his refusal to fill the space where our adult consciences must grow feels, at times, like absence.

For many Christians the connection between responsibility and absence becomes especially strong in their middle years. As we noted earlier, in midlife we find our parents aging and approaching death; we begin to prepare ourselves for their absence. Mentors and leaders once so compelling and directive in our lives are now less present to us. We taste absence in a variety of ways in midlife as we are gradually but surely orphaned of an older, authoritative generation. But this losing of parents and mentors creates the space for our own authority and leadership. Absence is the empty but fertile soil in which our midlife responsibility is compelled to grow.

This dynamic of human maturing—emptying our lives of others on whom we have relied so that we may become more reliable—is a frightening one. As a Christian people we have at times been tempted to deny or frustrate this maturing. The name of our major temptation is paternalism. As we discussed in Chapter Twelve, paternalistic tendencies tempt us to simplify the Christian community by dividing it between children and parents. Beginning with the graceful image of life together as a family, we have at times been tempted to distort this image: enforcing a static relationship between "parental" ministers (whether or not they are called "father") and a "childlike" laity, we turn a graceful image into the idol of paternalism. Paternalism fails in the way parenting sometimes does: by not letting the child grow up. By refusing to relinquish their role, parents deny their children the opportunity to mature. Paternalistic leaders (in the church and elsewhere) need the rest of the community to remain children. Care, begun in charity, ends in constraint.

Paternalism also fails by denying absence. In the simplified world of parent and child, there is no dangerous absence of authority. This void is filled by leaders who know what is best for us. Acting in God's stead, these leaders "fill up" the space that would ordinarily compel us to develop our own adult judgments. In such an environment, we need not face the rigors of personal responsibility or the possible failures that accompany adult choice. Encouraged to just do what we are told, we fail to mature into adult Christians.

Four Faces of Intimacy

Absence, as our religious tradition illustrates and our own experience confirms, is more than loss and emptiness. It can be a special mode of presence. It can even become a face of intimacy. This feature of absence may become clear when we recall four experiences of intimacy.

The first face of human intimacy is that of a parent and child. In the gaze of a loving parent we first learn to trust and to play. Psychologist D. W. Winnicott's study of the developmental aspects of play in small children illuminates this intersection of trust and play: in playing, the child learns "to be alone in the presence of another." This concentrated "aloneness" of the child at play is, in fact, a style of intimacy. And this is a mode of solitary attention that we will need in our adult prayer. In the earliest stage of life, presence and absence are already getting acquainted. The child also-learns another lesson of absence—that the parent cannot be ever-present. Through tantrums and much turmoil the child comes to grasp that love can survive absence.

As we grow into young adulthood we confront another face of intimacy: we are graced with friends, companions, and lovers. In our religious maturing, we become not only children of God but companions and disciples of Jesus Christ. In this new and adult style of presence we learn again about trust and play. And we are brought to new challenges—how to assertively express affection and commit ourselves in love. And here, too, absence is never far away: we know our lover can die; we fail friends and lose companions in many different ways. Even Jesus is likely to tell us, as he told his first followers, "'Where I am going you cannot come'" (John 13:33). The absence that disrupts our religious innocence and the conflicts that accompany any maturing commitment call us toward the third face of intimacy.

This face of intimacy is that of the contestant and wrestler. A love that survives romance will lead us into struggle; for love to mature and commitments to grow, we need to confront conflict and compromise. For Christians the consoling model for this special and hardy aspect of intimacy will be Jacob and his nocturnal wrestling with Yahweh (Genesis 32). God makes strange, even unacceptable demands as our vocations mature. If we always flee from these challenges or too easily capitulate, we cannot know this face of intimacy. As in our human loves and commitments, we need to learn how to fight fair—how to contest, and assert, and wrestle with lovers and colleagues. When we can do this, we inherit not only wounds (though these are plentiful) but a new resilience and strength in intimacy. We can be present to one another in hardier ways.

The unfolding of intimacy in Christian life draws us from child to lover to wrestler. And in all of these modes of presence lurks another, darker face of intimacy: absence. The child has to learn (or wallow in its illusion of omnipotence) that the parent cannot always be present and that the child can survive this absence. As friends and lovers we learn, unwillingly, the absence that is generated by disagreement, and separation, and death. As wrestlers we learn that the absence of agreement or harmony can evoke struggles that invigorate us, even as they wound us.

And finally, if we are truly fortunate, we can welcome absence as the fourth face of mature intimacy. A child or spouse who has died is absent, but in our grieving we struggle to hold them present now in a different way. Grief and memory bring us to be with them in a new way—in absence. And, as we have seen, even God sometimes

seems to desert us. We may lose our faith as its adolescent boundaries are broken by our adult experience: God is gone. Or less trau-
matically, in our prayer we may enter a desert of God's silence. But
as we mature we recognize that this is not the absence of someone
who never was. It is the absence of someone who is gone for a good
reason. "It is for your own good that I am going" (John 16:7).

With this insight we may come to befriend absence. We come
to tolerate it because it is, itself, a mode of presence. Another name
for such absence is solitude. In solitude we savor stillness and
absence. Less driven to plunge into noisy activities to distract us
from our aloneness, we allow ourselves to taste this mellow flavor
of presence.

Recently we conducted a workshop in which participants
explored their images of God's presence and absence. We offer here
an evocative image that one of the participants shared.

She sits in a garden in the late autumn. It is a fully harvested
garden, and little depressions mark the places where once carrots
and turnips and potatoes were found. The garden is empty, quiet,
devoid of life. But in the mellowness of this scene an expectation
arises: this place will one day hold seeds again; life will recur here.
But for now, this day and this season, it is time to be empty. It is
time to taste absence.

In our own experiences of solitude and absence, we have the
opportunity to recall in memory and to anticipate in hope the mysterious presence of God that we can hardly do without.

We live in a world of absence: we do not always know, clearly and thoroughly, what God would have us do. We are not accompanied by ever-present parents or infallible guides who can save us
from doubt or the need for debate and discernment. Absence, in its
various forms, is frightening, but it is unavoidable and even fruitful.
Since it was the milieu in which our ancestors encountered God, we
can trust it will be the same for us.

Reflective Exercises

Every life is marked with absence. In this final reflection we invite you to revisit several experiences of absence.

1. Recall a friend or companion who is no longer in your life—someone who has moved away or, perhaps, died. Savor the special blend of absence and presence that this recollection evokes. Create an opportunity to share with a close friend the feelings of presence and absence that this recollection brings to mind.

2. In another quiet moment, turn to your imagination for images of God's absence in your life. These may be scenes or phrases or tastes or moods that describe a time of crisis or a period of desolation. Take time to let these images present themselves; don't feel forced to "produce" something. It may be useful to take notes on the images that arise for you. After some time with this exercise, consider these different images. What does each tell you about the experience of absence in your own life with God—its pain, its mellowness, its promise?

Selected Bibliography

Brown, Peter. *Body and Society: Men, Women, and Sexual Renun-ciation in Early Christianity.* New York: Columbia University Press, 1988. A probing and respectful look at the historical factors shaping early Christian spirituality.

Brueggemann, Walter. *Interpretation and Obedience.* Minneapolis: Fortress Press, 1991. This distinguished Scripture scholar continues here his effective work in bringing themes of the Hebrew Scriptures to bear in the life of the Christian community today. See also his earlier book, *The Prophetic Imagination* (Minneapolis: Fortress Press, 1978).

Carmody, Denise Lardner. *The Virtuous Woman: Reflections on Christian Feminist Ethics.* Maryknoll, NY: Orbis Books, 1992. A provocative reflection on the implications for Christian spirituality and morality of the orientation and insights of feminist thought.

Donnelly, Doris. *Putting Forgiveness into Practice.* 5th edition. Nashville, TN: Abingdon Press, 1986. This valuable pastoral resource gives graceful assistance to the tasks of personal and social reconciliation.

Erikson, Erik. *The Life Cycle Completed—A Review.* Boston: Norton, 1982. Erikson reexamines his classic model of human development from the perspective of its final stage, wisdom in mature age. For his discussion of play, see *Toys and Reasons* (Boston: Norton, 1977).

Ferder, Fran, and John Heagle. *Partnership: Women and Men in Ministry*. Notre Dame, IN: Ave Maria Press, 1989. This challenging and practical book examines the sources of tension in pastoral relationships between men and women.

Fischer, Kathleen. *The Inner Rainbow*. New York: Paulist Press, 1983. This insightful consideration of the role of imagination in religious living continues to nourish those on the spiritual journey.

Koch, Carl, and Joyce Heil. *Created in God's Image: Meditating on Our Body*. Winona, MN: Saint Mary's Press, 1991. A valuable resource, offering information and prayerful exercises to support the essential spiritual task of befriending our bodies.

LaCugna, Catherine Mowry, ed. *Freeing Theology: The Essentials of Theology in Feminist Perspective*. San Francisco: Harper Collins, 1993. A splendid collection of essays displaying the profound pastoral significance of current feminist theological work.

Levinson, Daniel. *Seasons of a Man's Life*. New York: Knopf, 1978. In an examination of men at midlife, the author discusses the role of the "dream" as personal ambition. See also his forthcoming book, *Seasons of a Woman's Life.*

Mitchell, Kenneth, and Herbert Anderson. *All Our Losses, All Our Griefs*. Philadelphia: Westminster Press, 1983. A cogent discussion of the personal and social dimensions of grief, seen as a necessary companion on the spiritual path.

Sofield, Loughlan, Carroll Juliano, and Rosine Hammet. *For Wholeness: Dealing with Anger, Learning to Forgive, Building Self-Esteem*. Notre Dame, IN: Ave Maria Press, 1990. This fine pastoral resource assists the movements of emotional and spiritual maturity.

Tavris, Carol. *Anger—The Misunderstood Emotion*. New edition. New York: Simon and Schuster, 1989. In an eminently readable style, Tavris offers a synthesis of current psychological theory and research on anger. For a similarly helpful synthesis on current research concerning gender differences, see her book *The Mismeasure of Women* (New York: Simon and Schuster, 1992).

Vaillant, George. *The Wisdom of the Ego*. Cambridge, MA: Harvard University Press, 1993. An eminent psychologist discusses the range of positive coping strategies that support adult maturing; see also his important earlier work *Adaptation to Life* (Boston: Little, Brown, 1977).

Whitehead, Evelyn Eaton, and James D. Whitehead. *Christian Life Patterns*. New edition. New York: Crossroad Publishers, 1992. An exploration of contemporary spirituality, drawing on classic Christian themes in dialog with findings of current social and psychological research. For further discussion of "the sense of the faithful," see their book *Community of Faith: Crafting Christian Communities Today* (Mystic, CT: Twenty-Third Publications, 1992).

————. *The Promise of Partnership: A Model for Collaborative Ministry*. San Francisco: Harper Collins, 1993. This comprehensive look at shared ministry explores the relationship of personal power to leadership style and examines the interaction of women and men in ministry together. Their discussion of dynamics between men and women continues in *A Sense of Sexuality: Christian Love and Intimacy* (New York: Crossroad Publishers, 1994).

Wright, Wendy. *Sacred Dwelling: A Spirituality of Family Life*. New York: Crossroad Publishers, 1989. A compelling consideration of the spiritual implications of family life.

Index

About the Authors

Evelyn Eaton Whitehead is a developmental psychologist. She holds a doctorate from the University of Chicago. Her professional work focuses on issues of adult maturity, the dynamics of leadership, and the social analysis of community and parish life.

James D. Whitehead is a pastoral theologian and historian of religion. He received his doctorate from Harvard University. His theological interests concern questions of contemporary spirituality, ministerial leadership, and theological method in ministry.

The Whiteheads are consultants in education and ministry through WHITEHEAD ASSOCIATES, which they established in 1978. Their ministry serves dioceses and religious congregations in the United States and elsewhere; they contribute regularly to programs of ministry education, leadership development, and adult formation in faith.

The Whiteheads are associate faculty of the Institute of Pastoral Studies at Loyola University of Chicago, with which they have been affiliated since 1970. In 1992 they served as distinguished visiting professors at the Warren Center of the University of Tulsa in 1992. The Whiteheads currently live in South Bend, Indiana.

Books by the Whiteheads

Seasons of Strength:
New Visions of Adult Christian Maturing

Shadows of the Heart:
Spirituality of the Negative Emotions

Sense of Sexuality

Community of Faith:
Crafting Christian Communities Today

The Promise of Partnership:
A Model for Collaborative Ministry

Christian Life Patterns

The Emerging Laity

Marrying Well:
Stages on the Journey of Christian Marriage

Method in Ministry

Seasons of Strength is a probing, thoughtful and inspiring exploration of what it means to become an adult Christian. Invaluable as a text in adult education, this book is a steady resource for classroom use and personal reflection.

Richard Woods, OP
Professor of Theology
Institute of Pastoral Studies
Loyola University at Chicago

This is a book for everyone genuinely seeking wholeness and holiness. We use *Seasons of Strength* extensively—and intensively—with those involved in ministries of spiritual direction, faith community development, religious education, and parish leadership.

Emma Bezaire, SNJM
Kathleen Lichti, CSJ
Adult Spirituality Centre
Windsor, Ontario, Canada

I have had the opportunity to use these powerful images of a maturing Christian vocation with both lay and religious women and men in different parts of the world. These metaphors seem to enter with ease in conversation in many cultures. In fact, the Whitehead's text invites participants to bring their own "images and metaphors" into the conversation, encouraging new strengths to emerge in their own professional and ministerial lives.

Miguel Campos, FSC
Director of Multicultural and
International Affairs
La Salle University in Philadelphia

The participants in our degree program are all experienced ministers, many at a point of significant transition in their work or personal lives. *Seasons of Strength* is tailored for them. The context of the text provides substantive material for their theological reflection, as they pursue further studies and plan their future ministry.

Jeannette Lucinio, SP
Director, MA in Pastoral Studies
Catholic Theological Union
Chicago